CONTENTS

Frightful First World War

CONTENTS

Woeful Second World War

FRIGHTFUL
FIRST WORLD
WAR

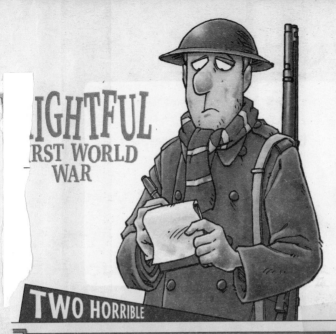

FRIGHTFUL
FIRST WORLD
WAR

TWO HORRIBLE

HORRIBLE HISTORIES

BOOKS IN ONE

WOEFUL
SECOND WORLD
WAR

TERRY DEARY · MARTIN BROWN

Scholastic Children's Books
Euston House, 24 Eversholt Street,
London, NW1 1DB, UK

A division of Scholastic Ltd
London ~ New York ~ Toronto ~ Sydney ~ Auckland
Mexico City ~ New Delhi ~ Hong Kong

First published in this edition by Scholastic Ltd, 2000
This edition published 2009

The Frightful First World War
First published in the UK by Scholastic Ltd, 1998
Text copyright © Terry Deary, 1998
Illustrations copyright © Martin Brown, 1998

The Woeful Second World War
First published in the UK by Scholastic Ltd, 1999
Text copyright © Terry Deary, 1999
Illustrations copyright © Martin Brown, 1999

All rights reserved

ISBN 978 1407 10907 7

Page layout services provided by Quadrum Solutions Ltd, Mumbai, India
Printed and bound by CPI Group (UK) Ltd, Croydon, CRO 4YY

11

Introduction

History can be horrible. So horrible that some boring old fogies think young people should not be told the whole, terrible truth.

But if you never learn the truth you'll miss out on some of the most useful things in life...

And the next time your new leather shoes hurt you, stuff them full of flowers. What happens? Nothing. The shoes stay hard and your feet get blisters.

Why couldn't your teachers tell you the truth about 'sweet pea' mixture? Either...

a) they don't know or

b) they know ... but they are too embarrassed to say.

What you need is a book that's not too embarrassed to tell you about the awful things people used to do. You want a history of the horrible.

And it's no use telling you...

That makes it sound cosy and peaceful, doesn't it? The truth is pretty nasty, but you'll never understand how those

7

people suffered unless you read their own true memories of trenches and no man's land…

> Bodies and bits of bodies, and clots of blood, and green metallic-looking slime made by the explosive gases were floating on the surface of the water. Our men lived there and died there within a few yards of the enemy. They crouched below the sandbags and burrowed into the sides of trenches. Lice crawled over them in swarms. If they dug to get deeper cover, their shovels went into the softness of dead bodies who had been their friends. Scraps of flesh, booted legs, blackened hands, eyeless heads came falling over them when the enemy fired shells at their position.

That's more like the truth because it was written by a soldier who was there.

Of all the history in the world the story of the First World War – also known as the Great War – is perhaps the most horrible. It's a story of what happens when machines go to war and human beings get in the way. But it's also a story of courage and craziness, brave people and batty people, friendships and fierce hatreds, love … and lice.

The Great War gangs

Why did the Great War start? Lots of big, thick history books have been written to answer that question. But, to put it simply, by 1914 the countries of Europe had formed themselves into two big gangs ... like street gangs. The gang called the 'Central Powers' were led by the Germans and the gang we call the 'Allies' were led by the French and British.

The two gangs started collecting weapons, making threats and swapping insults, the way gangs do.

All it needed was for one gang member to throw the first stone and a huge punch-up would follow.

The Black Hand bunglers

So exactly *how* did the First World War start? It's never one of the gang leaders that starts the fight, is it? It's always one of the scruffy little kids that hangs around the edge. In this case the scruffy little kid was called Bosnia in the Allies' gang.

And so a Serbian gang known as the Black Hand (honest!) waited till the Emperor came to Bosnia. Gavrilo Princip was a Serbian Black Hand freedom fighter.

NUMBER 2 SWALLOWED POISON AND JUMPED IN THE RIVER TO DROWN RATHER THAN BE CAPTURED

BUT THE CROWD DRAGGED ME OUT OF THE RIVER AND SAVED ME... THEN THEY NEARLY BEAT ME TO DEATH!

FERDI WENT TO THE TOWN HALL AND MADE A SPEECH. HE WAS IN REACH OF 3, 4, 5 AND 6. AND THEY...

ER... DID NOTHING

FERDI HEADED FOR THE HOSPITAL TO VISIT THE BOMB VICTIMS. BUT, BY AN AMAZING CHANCE, HIS DRIVER TOOK A WRONG TURNING. THIS ROAD BROUGHT HIM STRAIGHT PAST NUMBER 7...

ME! I JUMPED ON TO THE OPEN CAR AND FIRED TWO SHOTS...

I KILLED FERDI AND HIS WIFE. FERDI'S UNCLE, EMPEROR OF AUSTRIA, WAS FURIOUS. HE WANTED REVENGE AGAINST ALL OF SERBIA'S ALLIES. HE WANTED *WAR*

The first stone had been thrown. Austria declared war on Serbia, and Germany helped Austria so Russia helped Serbia so France helped Russia. Germany marched through Belgium to get to France so Britain helped Belgium.

The First World War had started. It was expected to last about four months but it lasted four frightful years.

But, before the war starts, here are two quick questions:

1 What happened to Ferdi's blood-soaked jacket after his death?

a) It was taken into battle like a flag for the Austrians to follow.

b) He was buried in it.

c) It was put in a museum, so gruesome people can go and gaze at it.

2 What happened to the assassin Gavrilo Princip?

a) He was shot by the police as he ran away.

b) He escaped and lived happily ever after.

c) He was arrested and put in prison.

Answers: **1c)** Franz Ferdinand's death was the start of the bloodiest war seen until that time. So his blood-soaked coat was an important reminder of the terrible event. It is now on display in the Austrian Historical Museum in Vienna. Go and see it ... if you like that sort of thing.

2c) Gavrilo Princip was taken alive. His two shots killed millions and millions of people. Yet he was allowed to live. Just as the First World War reached an end, gunman Gavrilo died in prison, of a lung disease. Pity it didn't get him four years before!

13

Wacky Willie

Things may have stayed calm and the Serbian trouble could have died down. But some of the leaders of the gangs weren't too bright and weren't too pleasant. Take the German monarch…

Title: Kaiser Wilhelm

Job: Monarch of Germany

Peculiarity: Unpopular. Nobody liked poor Willy. His grandmother, Queen Victoria of Britain, couldn't stand him. His (English) mother refused to wish him a happy birthday … so he sulked for days. His father thought he would be a dangerous leader – smart dad!

Weakness: He was born with a withered left arm and it embarrassed him. When he was photographed he insisted that he hide his weak arm. People around him hid their strong left arms too.

Nasty streak: German workers went on strike and he ordered soldiers to attack the strikers. 'I expect my troops to shoot at least 500,' he said.

Most likely to say: I hate everybody.

Least likely to say: Let's talk calmly about this.

1914 – The year of the first shot

No one is surprised when a war breaks out in August 1914. Germany smashed France in the Franco-Prussian War of 1871 and it was just a matter of time before France tried to take its revenge. But people are surprised that the war is still going on by the end of 1914. The two sides are like two heavyweight boxers jumping into the ring. Each one expects a quick knockout. But they will end up slugging it out, toe to toe, till they are exhausted.

Timeline 1914

28 June Archduke Franz Ferdinand is assassinated in Bosnia. Austria is very annoyed because he was going to be their next emperor. (Franz is too dead to be annoyed.)

23 July Austria blames Serbia for the death of Ferdi because the assassins were from Serbia. Serbia grovels but apology is not accepted. This means *WAR*.

4 August German army marches through Belgium to attack France, so Britain joins the war to help 'poor little Belgium'.

23 August Meanwhile, in the east, the German army defeats the Russian army. Round one to Germany.

9 September The French stop the Germans at the Battle of the Marne. Round two to France.

October Millions rush to join the armies. They're afraid it will be over before Christmas and before they can fight. It *will* be over before Christmas ... 1918.

22 November The Allies and the Central Powers have battered one another to a standstill in northern France. They dig 'trenches' opposite one another ... and won't move from them much for four years. No winners – only soldiers lose ... their lives.

25 December Enemies stop fighting for a day or two, and even play friendly football matches. It can't last, and it won't be repeated.

Did you know...?
The first Brits to fight in the First World War fought in London! On 2 August 1914, two days before war was declared, peace marchers clashed with Londoners who wanted war.

True lies

When you go to war you can't fight against nice people, can you? You have to believe the enemy are real slime-balls who would murder your granny and poison your gerbil if they won. You have to learn to *hate* them.

In Germany a new national anthem was written called the 'Hymn of Hate'. And when people met a friend in the street they no longer said, '*Güten Morgen*' (good morning) they said, '*Gott strafe England*' (God punish England). These words were rubber-stamped on letters, printed on millions of postcards, and engraved on badges and brooches.

Meanwhile, in the UK, the music of German composers was banned. (Since many had died some years before the war, they won't have been too upset.)

And if your enemy *wasn't* nasty enough, what could you do? You could invent a few lies about them. So, it was widely believed that German grocers in Britain had poisoned food and that German barbers were cutting their customers' throats and secretly dumping the bodies. Here's what the enemies said about one other … but can you spot the lies?

1 Brits believed the German soldiers were monsters…

IN BELGIUM BRITISH NURSES ARE BEING CARVED WITH KNIVES AND LEFT TO DIE IN BURNING HOSPITALS. AND GERMAN SOLDIERS HAVE BEEN THROWING UP BABIES, CATCHING THEM ON BAYONETS, ROASTING THEM AND EATING THEM

SO WHAT DO THEY TASTE LIKE SIR?

2 And the Germans believed the British were just as bad…

3 Germans believed foreign visitors were spies…

4 And the Brits didn't even trust their allies!

5 The Brits certainly didn't trust their own businessmen…

6 While the Germans knew who was to blame for starting the war…

7 The Germans also believed the most amazing tales of heroic deeds…

8 Brits were sure the Germans were desperate for materials and especially fat...

9 They were also sure that Germany was running short of fighting men...

Every one of these stories was believed – and every one was false, of course. Some were deliberate lies but others were simple mistakes. Take the story of corpses being melted to make oil. It appeared in a German newspaper report from the Western Front in April 1917...

We are passing the great Kadaver Exploitation Department of this Army Group. The fat that is won here is turned into lubricating oils and everything else is ground down in the bone mills into a powder which is used for mixing with pig's food – nothing can be permitted to go to waste.

Brits called corpses 'cadavers' and thought the Germans were melting *human* corpses. In German 'Kadaver' means an *animal* corpse. The corpses being melted down were horses.

The 'Fat King'

The Brits needed fat extractors too. Major Ellis – known to soldiers as the 'Fat King' – invented a 'fat extracting' plant and set it up on the French coast. This factory took waste food, dead horses and animal waste and turned it into fat. This was sent across the Channel to be made into glycerine – an important part of TNT explosives. Nine thousand tons of fat were produced by the 'Fat King's' factory.

So, a horse could be killed by a German shell (no, the army 'shells' were not like winkle shells you find on the beach. They were huge exploding bombs fired from large guns), turned into TNT and fired back at them! A perfect revenge!

WHY IS THE FAT KING LIKE A HORSE?

BECAUSE THEY BOTH ENJOY A LONG REIGN!

BOOM BOOM

Christmas crack-shots

The First World War was the first war to see aircraft used. To begin with they would fly over enemy armies and photograph their positions or bomb them. Then the defenders sent fighters to shoot down these spy planes. War in the air had begun.

Aeroplanes also meant Brits in their homes were no longer safe in a foreign war. Londoners discovered this after just four months…

LONDON DAILY RECORD 26 DEC. 1914

FOE FLIERS FLEE

Londoners had hopes of a quiet Christmas crushed when two German planes flew up the Thames yesterday. Crowds gathered in the streets to watch as two gallant airmen from our Royal Flying Corps chased the intruders at speeds of up to 70 miles an hour!

'I could hear the gunfire quite clearly,' a resident of Chiswick told our reporter. 'What if one of those bullets landed on an innocent head?' The aircraft observers had fired rifles at one another – a common sight in the skies over France these days. No one was hurt and the horrid Huns hurried back to Germany with their tails between their legs. But the use of guns is a deadly development of war in the air. In the early days of the war observers would carry a supply of bricks and try to drop one on to the enemy.

Londoners have been ordered to dim their lights this evening in case the unwanted visitors return. It has been reported that the Germans have invented steel darts to be dropped from their aircraft. If these strike a man they will split him in half from head to foot. Is there no end to the atrocious cruelty of this enemy?

'It just makes the people of Britain all the more determined to win,' a shop assistant from Wapping told our reporter. 'I am sending my Bobby down to the recruiting office today.'

The stories of brick bombs and deadly darts were true.

Later aircraft carried machine-guns; the pilot aimed his plane at the enemy and pulled the trigger. But there was a danger that the bullets would then hit his own propeller and shatter it. In time, engineers invented a timing gear so the bullets could only fire into the gaps between the turning propeller.

But how did the first machine-guns fire forward? If you were an Allied inventor, what simple solution could you come up with?

Answer: The propellers were covered with sheets of steel. If a machine-gun bullet happened to hit the propeller it bounced off.

Great idea – and it worked. For a month or two the German airmen were terrified and puzzled by the Allied fighter planes. Finally they captured one, saw how it was done and copied it.

The trouble is there was no way of telling where the bullet would bounce off to if it hit the propeller. It could smash into the pilot's own engine, if he was unlucky – or bounce back and hit him between the eyes if he was really, *really* unlucky!

Did you know…?

In the Second World War (1939–45) there were sirens to warn people of air raids. But when air raids became common in the First World War, many defence chiefs in Britain sent out a letter saying…

B7253A/6

It has been decided that no warning of air raids will be given as it is thought this may do more harm than good.

OFFICIAL

So, you could be walking to school and the first thing you know about the air raid is when you wake up dead.

Is this a record?

On 21 December 1914, William Gilligan, aged 41, joined the West Yorkshire Regiment at Hull. The next day, he deserted at York!

1915 – The year of total war

From 1915, battles are fought from trenches dug into the ground – where these battles are fought becomes known as the Western Front. Meanwhile the war spreads around the world. It is also the year of new weapons to kill new targets … including people in their homes!

People at home can't fight back but they can take it out on foreigners living in their country (known as 'aliens', but not to be confused with little green beings from Mars!). So, in the East End of London, German shops are looted and, in one riot, German pianos are thrown from houses onto the road. A street concert is held where patriotic songs are sung. The government is forced to imprison enemy aliens for their own protection as well as to stop them spying.

In Germany anyone with 'a well-cut coat, a well-filled wallet and a notably good car' is arrested as a spy. All British people are rounded up and most are imprisoned.

Timeline 1915

19 January First Zeppelin airship raids on Britain. Women and children, cats and dogs are in this war, like it or not.

2 February Germany says it will surround Britain with submarines, sink food supply ships and starve Britain to defeat.

18 March British Government asks women to sign up for war work. Many do and they start doing it better than the men did!

22 April Nasty new weapon,

poisoned gas, first used against soldiers in the trenches.

May Allies try to sneak round the back of the German front by landing in Gallipoli, Turkey. They expect the Turks will be a pushover.

7 May German submarines sink a passenger ship, the *Lusitania* – on board are 128 Americans who are not even part of the war yet. Big mistake, Germany.

7 June Zeppelin airship shot down over Flanders, northern France. That slow-moving bag of gas makes Zeppelins easy targets.

July The Turkish state uses war as an excuse to wipe out an entire race of people, the Armenians. A step on the road to the terrors of the Second World War.

August Food getting short, especially in Germany. Prices go up and taxes go up to pay for the war – £1 million a day in Britain is needed to pay for the fighting.

September At the Battle of Loos in Flanders some brave Brits dribble a football towards enemy lines. The ball was found riddled with bullets. Like the foolhardy footballers.

12 October Nurse Edith Cavell is caught helping Brit prisoners to escape in Belgium. She says, 'If I had to, I'd do it all over again.' Germans shoot her so she can't.

11 November Brit minister Winston Churchill gets sacked because his Gallipoli idea is a disaster. He'll be back.

20 December Allies give up on the Gallipoli attack and retreat. It was a very bloody mistake.

Pests and plagues

Soldiers had more to fear than enemy weapons. Creepy-crawlies and deadly diseases could kill you just as dead.

Fierce flies

At Gallipoli, flies in the summer of 1915 were very bad because of the number of unburied bodies. One soldier of the Australia and New Zealand Army Corps (Anzacs) wrote home about the flies…

Some of them must have tin openers on their feet, they bite so hard.

A Brit soldier complained…

In order to eat your food you had to wave your hand over it then bite suddenly, otherwise a fly came with it. Any bit of food uncovered was blotted out of sight by flies in a couple of seconds.

That fly had probably had a picnic on a dead donkey a few minutes before, so it's no wonder the troops suffered so much disease in Gallipoli.

Deadly doctors

Since Florence Nightingale's work in the Crimean War of 1856 it was a little safer in war hospitals. Back in Florie Nightie's day a wound could easily get infected – if the bullet didn't kill you then the germs did. But doctors could still be pretty clumsy. One soldier reported...

An Anzac soldier, Private O'Connor, was wounded in the leg and captured. He was taken to Istanbul where an Armenian doctor operated to amputate O'Connor's leg. The doctor sawed halfway through the bone, grew too tired, and snapped off the rest.

Frightful first-aid

In the middle of a battle you couldn't pop down to the local chemist shop for an aspirin or dial 999 for an ambulance. Soldiers had to look after each other and they all carried a small first-aid pack into battle. Brit soldiers also had a book, *The Field Almanac 1915*, that gave some advice.

There are some instructions you may *not* like to follow next time you are flattened in a fierce football match...

Broken limbs:
Gently put the broken limb straight after cutting off the clothes. Then fix it in this position by means of a splint made from a rifle, a roll of newspapers, bayonets, swords, pieces of wood.

A roll of newspapers! In a battle? What newspaper could be as tough as a wooden splint? The *Daily Telegraph-pole* perhaps?

By 1918, because of severe shortages in Germany, soldiers were forced to use bandages made from crêpe paper and tied on with thread.

F-f-f-f-frostbite

Frostbite is another problem you may suffer in school sports (especially during cricket matches in Britain). Again, you wouldn't want to suffer the 1915 cure…

Frostbite:
Carry the sufferer to a room or place without a fire, remove the clothes and rub hard with a cloth soaked in water or snow.

Brrrr!

And the way of preventing frostbite was even worse…

In the winter of 1914–15, anti-frostbite grease was supplied in 2 lb tins to soldiers on the Western Front. It looked like lard and it contained mostly pork fat. After 1915, whale oil was issued in rum jars. This was little used because of the terrible smell. Army orders said that, before going out on patrol in cold or wet weather, each man was to be stripped and rubbed down with whale oil by an officer. Most men refused to strip … and most officers refused to rub!

Putrid poisons

The army listed three types of poisoning. The emergency cure for 'corrosive' poisoning looks weird…

№ 31a   *British Army Field Almanac 1915*

Corrosive poisons:
Give scrapings from whitewashed walls or ceilings, mixed with water.

Perhaps the advice to eat walls is not so surprising. After all, Walls make great ice-cream and sausages!

Gruesome gas

A new First World War danger was gas attack. Orders went out from army headquarters…

If you are caught in a gas attack:
1 Take out your handkerchief.
2 Urinate into the material till it is soaked.
3 Tie it round your mouth and nose and breathe through it.

fig I

The orders didn't say what you should do if you didn't feel like a pee!

Crafty cordite

Soldiers wishing to appear unwell and thus avoid duty would chew cordite, an explosive taken from their rifle bullets. Cordite gave the soldier a high temperature but the effect soon wore off.

Lovely lice

At the Gallipoli battles the soldiers were forced to wear the same clothes for weeks without even taking them off. One Australian soldier finally got to take his socks off and saw a ghastly sight...

> And, Ma, I swear that as I dropped my socks on the floor I saw them start to move! They were a seething mass of lice!

In the trenches the soldiers found 'chatting' was a peaceful way to pass the quiet times. But 'chatting' didn't mean talking. It meant getting rid of the 'chats' or lice from the seams of their tunics.

One soldier compared lice to an army that had invaded his body...

The Little Soldiers of the Night
Though some hundreds you may kill,
Still you'll find there's hundreds still,
For they hide beneath each other
And are smart at taking cover;
Then you have an awful bite,
They've a shocking appetite.

31

> *There are families in dozens,*
> *Uncles, mothers, sisters, cousins,*
> *And they have their married quarters*
> *Where they rear their sons and daughters;*
> *And they take a lot of catching*
> *Cause an awful lot of scratching.*

German soldiers described another way of dealing with their bloodsucking friends. They took the lid from a boot polish tin and held it by a piece of wire over a candle. When the lid began to glow they'd simply drop the lice on the red hot tin. The sizzle of the frying lice was a sweet sound to their ears.

Did you know…?
British soldiers suffered from lice that were a pale fawn colour, but German soldiers had red lice. If they'd bred the two together they could have had pretty pink lice!

Seriously spooky

When your life is in danger then you start to believe in 'luck'. People in danger can be very superstitious. A few new beliefs sprang up in the First World War.

Super superstitions
Bullet-proof Bibles
Pocket-sized copies of the New Testament suddenly sold

tens of thousands of copies. They were being bought by anxious Brit mothers for their sons. There were stories of bullets being stopped by these little Bibles. There may have been one or two true cases of Bibles stopping 'spent' rifle bullets. They were not a lot of good against high explosive shells and machine-gun bullets.

God's people

Each side believed that they were in the right; that meant that God would be on their side. The Germans even went to war with a belt buckle that read, '*Gott mit uns*' (God with us). British soldiers saw the word '*uns*' and thought that proved what they knew – they were fighting the *Huns*! One very popular belief was that either God had your name and number on a bullet ... or he didn't. So, you may as well charge that machine-gun. After the war one soldier said...

I was most amazed by the bullets that missed *me!*

But the most dangerous superstition of all was that 'Prayer can turn bullets aside'.

For the soldiers who didn't believe in God or luck there was always this common sense advice. It was a notice passed around the trenches...

Don't worry

When you are a soldier you can be in one of two places:

A dangerous place or a safe place.

If you're in a safe place ... don't worry.

If you're in a dangerous place you can be one of two things:

One is wounded and the other is not.

If you're not wounded ... don't worry.

If you are wounded it can be dangerous or slight:

If it's slight ... don't worry.

If it's dangerous then one of two things will happen:

You'll die or you'll recover.

If you recover ... don't worry.

If you die ... you can't worry.

In these circumstances a soldier never worries.

The Third Man

NEVER LIGHT THREE CIGARETTES WITH A SINGLE MATCH

The reason for this belief was that it was a dangerous thing to do in the trenches where an enemy sniper might be watching.

First light will catch his eye, second light he'll fix his sights on the light and third light … he'll pull the trigger.

Mascots
Animals bring you luck. Regiments collected them as mascots: a bulldog mascot and the regiment is saying, 'We're tough'; a goat mascot says, 'We'll charge head-down and fearless.' What would your school mascot be?

But Bella and Bertha were an unusual choice for the Scots Guards. In late 1914, two cows were found near Ypres (pronounced 'ee-pruh' … though most Brit soldiers called it 'Wipers'), Flanders, by the regiment. They were the only survivors from a herd that had been hit by shell-fire. (Yeah, all the udders were dead.) The cows – soon named Bella and Bertha – became the battalion's mascots, providing fresh milk for the men in the trenches. After the war, the cows were taken to Scotland for retirement. When the Scots Guards marched through London on the Victory Parade, they were accompanied by Bella and Bertha.

The blasted statue
In the town of Albert, Flanders, there was a fine church with a golden statue of the Virgin Mary on top. Early in 1915 the tower was damaged and the statue toppled over

but didn't fall. For months it hung there as the war dragged on and the British defenders in Albert invented a strange superstition…

If the statue fell the British soldiers would be terribly discouraged, so the army set up strong cables to hold the Virgin Mary in her perilous place. For over three years the Germans failed to knock her off her perch and for three more years the war went on.

In 1918, the Germans finally captured the town and started using the top of the church tower as an observation post. From that high point they could guide their shell-fire towards the British. So it was the British who fired back and ended up demolishing the tower and brought the Virgin Mary down to Earth. The Germans were happy.

And, would you believe it? The war ended shortly after … but with the defeat of Germany.

Funny fact: After the British knocked the statue down it disappeared – probably sent to Germany to be melted down and turned into weapons.

When the war finished, Albert and its church were rebuilt. An exact copy of the statue stands there now. But ... it was suggested that the statue should be put back in her famous wartime pose!

The people of Albert said, '*Non!*'

Ghostly tales

With so many people dying in the First World War it's not surprising that ghosts were reported. In 1916, there was a great rise in 'spiritualists' – people who said they had the power to speak to the dead.

In late 1916 (after terrible losses at the Battle of the Somme where 20,000 Brits died on the first day alone) spiritualism became very popular in the UK with mothers trying to contact lost sons. Many fake spiritualists were caught and put in prison, but still the craze continued.

Why would a spiritualist lie to a woman about her dead son and pretend that she could speak to him? For money, of course. In December 1916, during the trial of fake spiritualist Almira Brockway, it was revealed that she was receiving over £25 a week for her work. Workers in the war factories worked 48 hours each week and made just £1.

Whenever there's misery and suffering you can be sure there is someone to cash in and make a fortune out of it. But some of the spooky stories are harder to explain than frauds and fakes. They are *seriously* spooky...

The angel army of Mons

In August 1914, British troops arrived in southern Belgium

to try and stop the German invasion. They were beaten back and slaughtered by the advancing enemy. Over 15,000 died in the early attacks. Yet some survived and reports said this was thanks to a miracle…

Arthur Machen, a journalist, turned the rumours into a short story. His story (called 'The Bowmen') said it was the English heroes of the 1415 Battle of Agincourt who had come to the rescue. (The battle was fought nearby.) Machen's story was published in the *London Evening News* a few weeks after the Battle of Mons and many Brits believed it. Some of the soldiers who returned from the battle then said it was true.

Even when Machen said he'd invented the whole story there were some people who went on believing in the angels.

Explanations: Some religious people have said the phantom army was made up of the spirits of the soldiers who had just died in the battle.

Some doctors believed that the Allied soldiers had hallucinations – waking dreams – because they were stressed by fear, pain and exhaustion.

But, weirdest of all, the German spy chief, Friedrich Herzenwirth, claimed that he had created the angels. He had sent up aeroplanes with cinema projectors. These projected images of angels on to the low clouds. He did this to encourage the German soldiers who would believe God was on their side.

The Montrose ghost
In October 1917, a ghost was seen at Montrose aerodrome in Scotland. One witness said…

> *It glided up to the door of the old aerodrome bar room and then vanished.*

It was seen several times afterwards by many officers. They were sure it was the ghost of Lieutenant Desmond Arthur who had been killed in a flying accident. Why was air-ace Arthur haunting the site of his crash?

An official enquiry had blamed the accident on Desmond Arthur himself. It said…

> He was killed by his own foolishness.

Yet the other officers knew that Lieutenant Arthur was a good pilot. They believed that his spirit was tortured by the insulting enquiry. Arthur's friends believed the ghost would not rest until his name was cleared by a second enquiry.

When this second enquiry decided…

We blame the fatal accident on a badly repaired machine.

…the ghost paid one final visit to the bar room in January 1917 and then was never seen again.

Explanations: Desmond Arthur's friends were angry that he was blamed for his own death. They started the rumours of the ghost to attract the attention of the newspapers. The fascinated public then demanded to know the truth and a second enquiry was ordered.

Or … the ghost seemed to spend a lot of time in the *bar room*. Did the 'spirits' they poured in their glasses, make the officers see 'spirits' walk through the door?

The spirit of the Somme

Soldiers in hospital enjoyed swapping stories of their experiences. Some of them were strange and mysterious…

Explanations: Soldiers would be bored in hospital. They could well get into a competition to tell the most exciting story. And, if their true stories weren't exciting enough, they could make one up! After all, it's hard to prove that the storyteller was lying.

Or ... the storyteller was led to safety by an officer who

looked like the dead officer. When the storyteller lost sight of the Captain he believed he'd seen a ghost.

Or … a ghostly captain went on protecting his men even after he'd died. He became their guardian angel.

The dead poet's footsteps

One of the most famous victims of the war was the poet, Rupert Brooke. He'd written a poem about the glory of war. (This was a dumb thing to do since he'd never seen the horror of it, but the people back in Britain wanted to believe him.)

If I should die think only this of me:
That there's some corner of a foreign field
That is forever England.

Rupert used to live in Grantchester Vicarage near Cambridge, and he wrote another famous poem about it. (The poem is called 'The Old Vicarage, Grantchester' … no prizes for guessing why.)

He was sent off to fight in Gallipoli but never made it. In April 1915, he was bitten on the lip by an insect and died of blood poisoning. (It must have been a dirty insect that forgot to clean its biting teeth. This was probably *not* the glorious end Rupert imagined.) The 'corner of a foreign field that is forever England' is his grave in an olive grove on the Greek Island of Skyros, by the way.

When the war was over a doctor called Copeland moved into Rupert's old rooms in Grantchester Vicarage. One frosty evening he sat reading by the fire with his bulldog at his feet…

Suddenly the dog woke up and growled at the window. In the silence that followed I heard slow, regular footsteps coming round the house and heading for the window! I threw open the window ... and there was no one there!

GRRRR

Doctor Copeland's landlord explained that the footsteps had been heard ever since Rupert Brooke was killed four years before. (His phantom feet must have been hurting a bit by 1919!)

Explanations: The dog heard burglars.

Or ... Rupert didn't like being stuck in 'some corner of a foreign field' and wanted to come home.

Or ... the owners of Grantchester Vicarage wanted to believe that their famous lodger still remembered them. But isn't it strange that only the 'famous' Rupert Brooke came back and not some ordinary Joe Blogg?

Or ... maybe it isn't Rupert's ghost after all. Maybe it *is* Joe Blogg's ghost! This is not as silly as it sounds. In Grantchester churchyard there is a memorial for the local men who died in the First World War. There are usually flowers at the foot of the memorial, put there by poetry lovers who remember the famous Rupert. Is that fair?

What about the other brave men who died? Are they forgotten and do they return to haunt the Vicarage in revenge? Look carefully at the memorial and you will see half a dozen other names on there. And one of the other (forgotten) names is … 'Joseph Blogg'.

Simple spymen

Some places were haunted long before the First World War. But the war brought them new horrors and new ghosts. Take the ancient Tower of London, for example. The war brought it back into use in a horrible historical way…

Terror in the Tower

'Have you any last requests?' the Major asked the young man in the shabby black suit.

'I have, good sir. I would like to play my violin one last time. Before you shoot me.'

The Major nodded and opened a hatch in the steel door and called to the guard outside, 'Bring Herr Buschmann's violin from the office.' He turned back to the prisoner. 'You are honoured, young Fernando. You will be the first to be executed in the Tower of London for hundreds of years.'

The young man gave a faint smile. 'It is a greater honour to die for Germany,' he said.

'It would be better to *live*,' the Major pointed out and pulled a wooden chair to the side of the bed and sat facing the German spy.

'My wife and child will suffer back in Germany. I regret being caught … but I do not regret spying for my country,' he said calmly.

The Major shook his head sadly. 'It was Germany that sent you here to die.'

'No, they sent me here to *spy*.'

'But they prepared you so badly we were *bound* to catch you!' the Major groaned. 'Don't you see that?'

'No,' the prisoner frowned.

The officer leaned forward and lowered his voice. 'You will die at dawn, so there is nothing to lose by telling you this, Fernando. But they trained you in the spy school at Rotterdam. The head of the spy school is Herr Flores.'

'Perhaps.'

'We *know* it is!' the Major sighed. 'And he sent you here with a passport written in his own handwriting. We recognized it at once.'

For the first time a small frown of uncertainty crossed the young German's face. The Major went on. 'He sent you to a hotel in the Strand where he sends *all* of his secret agents. He gave you a cover story – you were to say you were a salesman of cheese, bananas, safety-razors and potatoes … but you know hardly anything about those things!'

The spy lowered his head a little in an admission of defeat. 'I sent in reports the best I could,' he muttered.

'You sent in reports that said we switch on London searchlights at eight p.m. and switch them off again at 10:30 if no Zeppelins appear,' the officer said. 'That is no great secret to die for.'

'You know what messages I sent?'

45

'Of course! You sent the messages in code to a school-master in Holland. That schoolmaster is a *British* spy. You were an amateur, Fernando. *We* will shoot you ... but it is *your* spy-masters who sent you to your death.'

There was a rap on the door and a guard handed a violin to the Major who passed it across to Fernando Buschmann. For the next three hours the sweet, mournful tones echoed round the ancient walls and stirred the ghosts of long-dead prisoners.

Slowly the sky lightened through the barred window and hobnailed footsteps clattered in the corridor outside. The prisoner played one last melody but now the notes were wavering and disconnected. 'Nice tune,' the Major said.

'By Pagliacci,' the German said. 'The music tells the story of a broken-hearted clown. Maybe that's all I was, Major.' He raised the violin to his lips and kissed it. 'Goodbye, I shall not want you any more.' He laid his precious instrument on the hard bed, straightened his back and faced the men who waited at the door. 'I am ready,' he said.

Fernando Buschmann faced an eight-man firing squad on the morning of 19 October 1915. He refused a blindfold, saying he wanted to die like a gentleman. He was one of 11 bungling, amateur German spies to die in the Tower during the First World War. A 12th was hanged at Wandsworth Prison.

On 13 November 1997 the papers connected with the case were sold at an auction in London. The saddest was the letter from his wife to his lawyer Henry Garrett that read...

Dear Mr Garrett

I would be grateful if you could send me details of my husband's last moments. Was he at least allowed to keep his violin till his last hours? Had he much to suffer? Will I find his tomb in London to weep at it? My only wish is to visit and to sleep there where my beloved husband is sleeping...

There were many ways to die, and many wasted lives, in the First World War. Fernando Buschmann's was just another one.

Awful agents

In the years before the First World War Britain was overrun with German spies because they guessed this war would come one day. It wasn't till 1908 that Britain had any spy-catchers – the Secret Service Bureau.[1] Captain Vernon Kell

1. In 1916 this was renamed Military Department 5 – the famous MI5. By the end of the war it had 844 members.

was the only member of the Secret Service Bureau and by the start of the war in 1914 he had only nine officers. The Bureau did such a good job that they arrested 21 agents as soon as the war began.

The Bureau had a lot of help from the German spies who were not too clever. In fact, they were awful agents. They got their information from Germans working in Britain – hairdressers and pub landlords were favourites because they heard lots of gossip. And German teachers were a bit treacherous too! (Would you trust a teacher?)

Their code words included...

- eggs = foot-soldiers
- condensed milk = horse soldiers
- margarine = guns
- Dutch cheese = battleships
- tinned lobster = torpedo boats

Now that code may be hard to crack (except 'eggs' which are easy to crack) but you don't have to be James Bond to solve the following genuine German code. Match the code to the real meaning ... the simple spymen left enough clues in the choice of words!

1 Floating down	a) Dartmouth Naval Base
2 Old folks at home	b) Destroyers
3 Dark melodies	c) Old battleships
4 Chattanooga Rag	d) Southampton
5 Down South	e) Submarines
6 Pirates of Penzance	f) Chatham Base

TOP SECRET

That was too easy. So try this quick quiz…

Sly spy
Which of the following statements are true?
1 MI5 agents used girl guides to carry their messages … but the girls had to promise not to read them.

2 An American (spying for Germany) was arrested as soon as his socks were tested. When they were soaked in water they produced invisible ink.

3 A German spy put up a poster in Portsmouth offering £5

49

to anyone who would give him information about the warships there.

4 British spies in Germany were told, 'If someone starts taking an interest in you then you will end up having to kill him. So don't waste time. Do it.'

Answer: The above statements are all totally ridiculous. And they are all totally *true*. Girl guides *were* used to carry messages (because they proved more reliable than boy scouts) and Brit agents in Germany really were 'licensed to kill'. In November 1997 MI5 published the secret files at last and these wacky facts came to light.

1916 – The year of the Somme

In 1914 millions of men had rushed to join their armies and fight for their countries. By 1916 they are trained and ready and are sent off to fight the biggest battle ever. The battleground is around the river Somme in northern France.

This is to be the battle that ends the war for good! All it does is end the war for the million or so captured, wounded or killed. For the rest it goes on … and on and on…

Timeline 1916

25 January 'Conscription' comes to Britain. That means fit, single men *have* to join the army whether they like it or not.

February The French and Germans begin the longest battle of the war, at the fortress of Verdun in north-eastern France. Even Big Bertha (that's a gun firing one-ton shells, not a woman) can't win it for the Germans.

March German soldiers are told to have one day a week without food to save on supplies … but the officers seem to eat well *every* day!

24 April The Irish rebel against British rule and try to seize Dublin *Post Office*! Brits soon *stamp* that out!

May The only great sea battle of the war takes place at Jutland.

Germans claim victory but never try to fight the Brit navy again.

5 June Lord Kitchener's face is on a million posters saying 'Your country needs YOU!' Today he dies when his ship hits a mine.[1]

1 July The Battle of the Somme begins. Today Brits outnumber Germans seven to one ... but lose seven men to every one German. Very bloody draw.

10 August A frightful news film, *The Battle of the Somme*, is shown in Brit cinemas even though it's not over yet. It's seen by 20 million shocked Brits.

15 September New Brit super-weapon, the 'Willie', enters the war. Luckily someone has changed its name to the 'Tank', giving rise to a horrible historical joke. Question: There were two flies in an airing cupboard. Which one was in the army? Answer: The one on the tank.

October In a Brit election the 'Peace' candidate is heavily defeated by the one supporting the war. For all the bloodshed, Brits back home still don't want peace.

1. In 1930 a German spy-master said that *he* arranged to have Kitchener killed. He claimed he got Irish enemies of Britain to sneak a bomb on board Kitchener's ship, then he watched from the shore as the bomb was detonated. Don't believe him. It was a mine!

14 November End of the Battle of the Somme. Allied and German losses – over 1.3 million men. Allied gains – six miles. That's 120 men for every yard of ground won. Expensive ground.

7 December Lloyd George becomes new Brit prime minister. Old prime minister Asquith says, 'I distrust him.'

Silly (but true) story

In the great Somme advance of 1 July 1916 a soldier was given the job of taking a messenger pigeon in a basket to the front. He was told that an officer would use it to send a message when the first target was reached.

Back at headquarters they waited hours and hours for the pigeon and finally it appeared. The anxious commander cried, 'Give me the message!' and it was handed to him.

He opened it and read, 'I am absolutely fed up with carrying this bloody bird around France.'

Daft DORA

Who was DORA? DORA was Britain's Defence of the Realm Act. And DORA could be *very* fussy.

The people of Britain had to live by DORA's rules.

But which rules? Here are some strange regulations. But which are real DORA rules and which are real daft rules?

DEFENCE OF THE REALM ACT

YOU MUST NOT

1... loiter under a railway bridge
2... send a letter overseas written in invisible ink
3... buy binoculars without official permission
4... fly a kite that could be used for signalling
5... speak in a foreign language on the telephone
6... ring church bells after sundown
7... whistle in the street after 10pm for a taxi
8... travel alone in a railway carriage over the Forth Bridge
9... push a handcart through the streets at night without showing a red light at the back and a white light on the front
10... eat sweets in the classroom

One rule which upset children was the one that said, 'You must not keep fragments of Zeppelins or bombs as souvenirs'. All children hunted for these and ignored the law.

What's a Zeppelin? A huge German airship that flew over Britain and dropped bombs on cities. No one in Britain had ever suffered this sort of attack before and some people feared the dangers a bit too much.

Zeppelin Zep-panic

DORA ordered that no lights could be shown after dark. In 1916, in York, the first person fined was Jim Richardson, who was fined five shillings for lighting a cigarette in the street at night. The Zep-panicking magistrate told him that a lighted match could be seen by a Zeppelin flying 2,000 feet up.

The Rev Patrick Shaw was arrested for showing a light from his church, despite his plea that it was only a 'dim religious light'. The Zep-panicking magistrate fined him anyway.

Police also banned loud noises. In York, the Chief Constable told residents...

Do not laugh in the street, stop your dogs barking and do not bang doors because all these noises can be heard from a Zeppelin listening for its target.

The man was clearly a Yorkshire *pudding*! But was he any worse than the newspaper which had the bright idea to light a huge area of empty countryside at night to attract Zeppelins and then destroy them – like moths around a candle flame!

Foul food and worse water

If you think school dinners are bad then you should be glad you didn't live in Europe in 1914–18. It's hard to tell if the food and drink was worse at home or in the army.

Would you like a cup of tea in the trenches? Or would you prefer a drink of milk in your wartime home?

You'd like tea in the trenches? Well, the soldiers' water had chloride of lime added to kill the germs in it. The trouble was the chloride of lime made the water taste *terrible*, even when it was boiled and used to make a cup of tea. It's a bit like drinking your local swimming-bath water. Yeuchy. So, would you prefer...

Milk at home? In London, William Saxby, a milkman, was sentenced in 1917 to two months' hard labour for selling his customers milk watered down with 'foul water obtained from a public lavatory basin'. Yeuchier!

Rotten rations

British soldiers were offered a delightful tinned stew called Maconochie. A joke recipe appeared in a soldiers' newspaper. Sadly it was close to the truth!

Maconochie Hotpot

1 Open one tin of Maconochie rations.

2 Warm gently until the greasy oil floats to the top. Remove this by blotting it up with a piece of flannel. (Place this on one side for later use.)

3 Remove the black lumps from the tin. These are potatoes.

4 Squeeze the greasy oil from the flannel into a frying-pan and gently fry the potatoes.

5 Take two handfuls of dried vegetables (they look like any other dead leaves). Mix with water flavoured with chloride of lime and pat into a pancake. This should be gently fried after the potatoes.

6 Heat up the remains of the stew, then serve with the potatoes and vegetables on a cold enamel plate.

Soldiers were also given bully beef (like corned beef) to which they liked to add raw onions. Sometimes they had to eat this with hard biscuits.

The French peasants who gave rooms to British soldiers were glad of these biscuits ... they made excellent fire-lighters!

Jam was usually plum and apple and arrived in the trenches in tins. Empty tins made useful home-made grenades!

Young soldiers suffered badly. Ernest Parker, a soldier in the 10th Battalion of the Durham Light Infantry, said…

Army food was monotonous and in the trenches bully beef and bread, often without butter or jam, was the usual fare. Teenagers like myself were always hungry. Alas, when we needed food most it sometimes did not arrive at all, and it was far from pleasant to spend 24 hours or more in the front line with nothing to eat. Sometimes when drinking water did not arrive, we were driven to boiling water from shell holes and this may account for the crop of boils and diarrhoea that plagued us.

Apart from the bully beef and the Maconochie the soldiers had two other big food complaints…

One was the cakes that friends and family sent from home! Deadlier than a German bullet some soldiers reckoned.

The other pet hate is explained in a popular poem of the time…

Fear

A terror hangs over our heads,
I scarcely dare to think
Of the awful doom that each one dreads
From which the bravest shrink.
It's not the crashing shrapnel shell,
It's not the sniper's shot,
It's not the machine-gun's burst of Hell,
These matter not a jot.
It's a far worse thing than that, son,
With which we have to grapple.
It's if we see another one
More tin of Plum and Apple.

Horse sense

The Allied soldiers complained but it was even worse for the German army. One tip sent to the soldiers read...

> For tender roast horse flesh, you should boil it first in a little water, before you put it in the roasting pan.

But they only ate horses for the *mane* course.

Suffering civilians

British people may have gone hungry from time to time. But the people of Germany were starving for most of the First World War.

As early as 1915 'Eat less' posters appeared all over Germany with the 'Ten food commandments'. These included...

No.7 Do not cut off a slice of bread more than you need to eat. Think always of the soldiers in the field who would rejoice to have the bread which you waste.

Belly laughs

The British people believed that the Germans would be starved into defeat. In 1914 Germany only produced 80% of its food, 20% had to be imported, so the blockade of Germany by the Royal Navy caused severe shortages and suffering.

By the end of the war Germans *were* starving, but in September 1915 they could still laugh about the British blockade. That month a Zeppelin raid on London dropped 70 bombs, killing 26 people and wounding almost 100. But the crew also dropped a ham bone attached to a parachute. On it was written, 'A gift from starved-out Germany'.

By September 1918, the German people had stopped laughing ... and they didn't have spare ham bones for jokes.

Hunger horrors

We all know what it's like to be hungry, but very few of us in Europe today know what it's like to be *really* starving, year after year.

Maybe you could try this diet for just *one day* and see how it feels. (Get your friends to sponsor you and give the money to a good cause.) Then remember this is how most Germans ate in the winter of 1916–1917 on a *good* day. It was known as the Turnip Winter because turnip was the only food that was plentiful.

The Turnip Winter diet

You need:
six slices of bread
50g of meat
two teaspoons of sugar
two teaspoons of coffee
50g of cheese
one cup of soup
vegetables (half a turnip, handful of peas, beans, mushrooms, nuts), half a cup of blackberries

Breakfast
Two slices of bread (no butter), one cup of coffee with a spoonful of sugar but no milk

Lunch
Soup with meat and turnip chopped in, peas and beans added. Cup of coffee, two slices of bread

Supper
Cheese, two slices of bread, water

Snacks
Nuts and berries

And, now, the *bad* news...
- You would only have the mushrooms, nuts and berries if you'd gone out and picked them in the autumn. (You might have to fight the squirrels for the juicy ones!)
- The meat would probably be horse or dog. (After a day of

the Turnip Winter diet you may look at your pet poodle and lick your lips.) Even the kangaroos in the German zoos were killed and eaten.

- You might not even be able to get dog meat. In April 1916, all Berlin butchers were closed for five days because they had no supplies of anything. In July 1916, women demonstrated outside the Town Hall in Dusseldorf demanding more meat and potatoes. When the Mayor offered them more beans and peas, they rioted and smashed every window in the Town Hall.
- Cream was only obtainable on a doctor's prescription.
- The German newspapers tried to calm things down – one published a long article proving that overeating was the cause of baldness!
- By late 1916, women queued outside food shops all night, bringing camp stools, knitting, etc. (One woman was seen in a queue with a sewing machine to pass the time.)

Hot chestnuts

While Germans were starving, Brits were getting ready for the day when they would have to live with less food. In January 1918, this poster appeared…

Healthy advice even today. But some of the recipes look as tasty as a can of vegetarian cat-food.

The National Food Economy League Book of War-time Recipes had this recipe that you may like to try if you really want a taste of the First World War (or if you are the sort of dustbin that would swallow anything).

Chestnut curry
You need:
one pound chestnuts; 1/2 to 3/4 pint curry sauce
Method:
1 Slit and boil the chestnuts for 20 minutes. Remove both outer and inner skins very carefully. (To do this, leave in the hot water and peel one by one.)
2 Place in a casserole with curry sauce (made from a tablespoon of curry powder and a tablespoon of flour in 3/4 pint of water).
3 Put in a medium oven to simmer for two hours, until the chestnuts have taken up all the water and are thoroughly tender.
4 Serve with plain, boiled rice.

No wonder the Brits sang...

My Tuesdays are meatless,
My coffee is sweetless,
Each day I get poorer and wiser.
My home it is heatless,
My trousers are seatless,
My God, but I do hate the Kaiser.

But by 1916 it wasn't only the Brits who hated the Kaiser. The Germans were beginning to turn against him. And no wonder. If food was bad in Britain it was worse in Germany...

Fake food

All Germans who lived through the First World War remembered not only the lack of food but the frightful food *substitutes* that they were forced to eat – known as 'ersatz' food. As the war dragged on, exhibitions were held all over Germany to demonstrate the huge range of ersatz food and drinks, for example...

Bread soon contained flour made from beans and peas, and often sawdust was added.

Cakes were made from clover and chestnut flour.

Meat was replaced by the rice lamb chop or the vegetable steak (pale green, made from spinach, spuds, ground nuts and eggs substitute).

Butter was 'stretched' with starch or made from a mix of curdled milk, sugar and yellow colouring.

Eggs were made from a mix of maize and potatoes.

Pepper was 'stretched' with ashes.

Fats – many attempts were made to make fats: from rats, mice, hamsters, crows, cockroaches, snails, worms, hair clippings, old leather boots and shoes. None of those was very successful.

Coffee was first made from roast nuts flavoured with coal tar – with sugar this was OK! Later came coffee–ersatz–ersatz – roasted acorns or beech nuts. Later still, when all acorns had to be fed to pigs, came coffee made from carrots and turnips.

Horrible? At least they filled the stomach. By late 1918, even ersatz foods had run out. For German soldiers struggling to fight, a meal might be turnip stew served with chunks of turnip bread.

Hungry people lose the will to fight. Germans lost that will – the Allies, who hadn't suffered nearly so much, did not lose their will. It's one of the reasons the Germans lost. It was also a reason why the Germans felt so bitter at losing. All that pain for nothing. Ten years after the First World War ended that bitterness drove them to support Adolf Hitler and a second war.

1917 – The year of the mud

The winter of 1916–17 is bitterly cold, but especially for the French. The Germans hold the north-west where most French coalmines are. One jeweller in Paris places a small lump of coal surrounded by diamonds in his window.

Houses in Paris are allowed only one electric light in each room (anyone caught with more will have their electricity cut off for three weeks!).

In Germany coal is just as short. Berlin lights are to be put out by nine p.m. Elephants from the circus are used in Berlin to pull coal carts from the railway stations – it saves wasting coal on steam trains or using horses that could be working in the army. German workers go on strike while French soldiers have their own rebellion. Everyone is desperate for peace – but the war goes on … and on.

Timeline 1917

January A munitions factory blows up in Silvertown, East London, killing 69.

February The Russian people rebel against their leaders and Russian soldiers lend their rifles to help the revolution. Good news for Germany.

March In Britain the Women's Army Auxiliary Corps (WAAC) is founded and a new joke is born…

April The Doughboys are here! No, not bakers' men, but American soldiers as the USA joins the war.

Meanwhile French troops rebel against their conditions.

May UK horse-racing stopped, followed by county cricket and league football.

June Brit ban on rice being thrown at weddings and feeding birds – food is too precious.

July The war now costs Britain nearly £6 million a day. Will they run out of money or men first?

1 August Terrific rain storms as the British attack in Flanders. The mud is as deadly an enemy as the Germans.

4 September German submarines shell Scarborough. Why shell a seaside holiday town when it has a beach full of shells?

October Brit bakers allowed to add potato flour to bread while French bread has become grey, soggy stuff.

November War between Russia and Germany coming to an end as the Russian 'Bolsheviks' start to take over their country.

6 December German Giants reach London. (They're bomber aircraft, not monster men.) They're harder to catch than the old Zeppelins.

Wild Western Front

From November 1914 the two huge armies dug trenches in the ground and faced one another in a line from Belgium to Switzerland. From time to time one tried to attack and push back the other. The defenders usually won in the end ... but only after both sides had lost large numbers of men.

Lots of books have described trench life on the Western Front. The soldier's only comfort was that it was just as bad for the enemy as it was for himself. Here are six descriptions of trench life from Allied or Central Power soldiers. But which are which?

1 Which side suffered disgusting trenches?

Lice, rats, barbed wire, fleas, shells, bombs, underground caves, corpses, blood, liquor, mice, cats, filth, bullets, fire, steel; that is what war is. It is the work of the devil.

2 Which side fought till they were exhausted skeletons?

There were about 20 men. They walked like living plaster statues. Their faces stared at us like those of shrunken mummies, and their eyes seemed so huge that one saw nothing but eyes. Those eyes, which had not seen sleep for four days and nights showed the vision of death. Was this the dream of glory that I had when I volunteered to fight?

3 Which side fought because they thought it was their duty to God and that he was on their side?

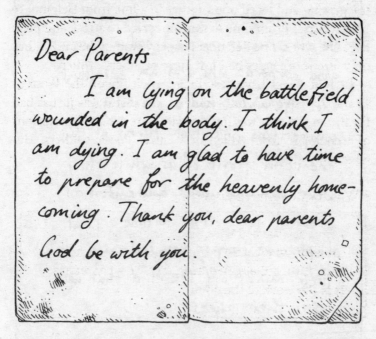

Dear Parents

I am lying on the battlefield wounded in the body. I think I am dying. I am glad to have time to prepare for the heavenly home-coming. Thank you, dear parents God be with you.

4 Which side believed that its heavy shells would destroy the enemy trenches so all they had to do was walk across no man's land and take over?

For some reason nothing seemed to happen to us at first. We strolled along as though walking in the park. Then, suddenly, we were in the midst of a storm of machine-gun bullets and I saw men beginning to twirl round and fall in all kinds of curious ways as they were hit – quite unlike the way actors do it in films.

5 Which side sometimes shot the enemy as a sport?

We did some sniping. I had a very good corporal who was an excellent shot. He and I had a shooting competition. We took turns at the enemy in front of us while they were running about and moving around from time to time. That kept our troops amused and took their minds off the mud that was up to their knees.

Terrible toilets

A German writer described the pleasures of being out of the front line. What would you do to relax? Sleep? Write letters to your family? Clean your toenails? Not Erich Maria Remarque, the author of the famous book, *All Quiet on the Western Front*, who said that...

> *The experienced soldiers don't use the unpleasant, indoor, common toilet, where 20 men sit side by side in a line. As it is not raining, they use the individual square wooden boxes with carrying handles on the sides. They pull three into a circle and sit there in the sun all afternoon, reading, smoking, talking, playing cards.*

In the front line trenches it was different and more dangerous. There were no toilets in the Brit trenches, just buckets. If you upset the Sergeant you would be given the job of taking the buckets out after dark. Your job was to dig a hole and empty the buckets. Once you were out of the cover of the trenches you were in danger, but some soldiers still lit cigarettes to hide the smell from the buckets. Enemy snipers were just waiting to aim at the glow of a cigarette end. Emptying toilet buckets could be bad for your health.

THAT ROTTEN SNIPER HIT ME RIGHT IN THE BUCKETS

Even *going* to the toilet shed just behind the trenches was dangerous. The enemy knew men used these toilets at dawn and liked to drop a few shells among the toilet huts to catch the soldiers with their pants down!

Terrible toilet tale 1…
A major found some deserted houses for his men. He looked at the sign at the end of the street and copied it carefully. Then he sent a message to his soldiers…

You will find rooms in "Verbod te wateren"

Unfortunately, he couldn't read Flemish and didn't understand that the sign *wasn't* the street name. It was a warning notice that said, 'You must not pee in the street'.

Terrible toilet tale 2…
Army boots had to be tough. The trouble was the leather was so hard it gave men blisters. Old soldiers knew the answer…

You probably won't want to try this with your new school shoes. But, if you do, remember to *empty* them before you put them on!

Terrible toilet tale 3…

In the 1917 battles in Flanders the troops didn't have properly built trenches, just shell holes protected by sandbags. And there were certainly no toilet huts. One officer complained…

> *If you wanted to do your daily job of urinating and otherwise there was an empty bully-beef tin, and you had to do that in front of all your men, and then chuck the contents (but not the bully-beef tin) out over the back.*

He forgot to mention one important thing. Find out which way the wind is blowing first!

Frightful fun and gruesome games

If you grew bored with 'chatting' you could always try one of the violent entertainments that soldiers used to pass the time…

Games you wouldn't want to play

1 Free the prisoner (Australian Rules)

To play:
- a grenade
- a German prisoner

The rules:

First find a prisoner who wants to go free. Take him to the gates of the prison and place a hand grenade in his back pocket. Pull the pin out of the grenade (which will explode in five seconds). Hold the prisoner for a count of 'One – two', then release him and tell him to run. If he gets the grenade out of his pocket in the remaining three seconds he is the winner and is free to go. If he gets the grenade out of his pocket and throws it back at you then you are the losers. But that's the risk you take.

There are reports of this happening, so it is probably true, but extremely rare.

2 Beetle racing

You need:
- two or more beetles
- a table
- sugar
- matchsticks

To play:

Each 'jockey' chooses a beetle and holds it at one end of the table. A sugar lump is placed at the other end of the table to attract the beetles. Every jockey places one matchstick on the table. On a signal, the beetles are released. The first beetle to reach the sugar wins and the winning jockey collects everyone else's matchsticks. (And the beetles get to eat the sugar.)

3 Sea swimming

You need:

• the sea

To play:

At Gallipoli the chief hobby for Anzac troops was swimming. This took a lot of courage because the Turkish army were shelling the beaches. Troops swam for fun and to keep cool (but also because there was no water for washing in the trenches). Beaches were somewhat spoilt by the sight and smell of dead horses, mules and donkeys.

4 Barge boating

You need:

• a wooden box
• two shovels

In 1917, as Sergeant Ernest Parker was sitting reading at the entrance to his dugout in the banks of the Yser canal, he saw an exciting regatta…

Lustily plying two oars, a ruffian member of my band was propelling a rectangular box up and down the canal. Shovels were the oars and when rival craft were launched a naval battle began, cheered by the spectators, who were hoping that somebody would take a plunge into the black slime of the canal.

Weird words

If you were a British soldier in the First World War you would soon learn a new language – army slang. In fact, there were *two* languages to learn – one used by the officers and one by the ordinary soldiers.

Could you learn to 'sling the bat' (speak in the local language, that is) with the soldiers or the officers?

Batty bat slinging
What would you do if someone came up to you and said…

Of course that will all make perfect sense to you. No? Oh, well, here's an explanation…

1 I'd love some nice meat pudding followed by bread and cheese, washed down with a cup of strong tea. For afters I'd like jam on bread.

2 Now, my good man, this afternoon (p.m.) we need some tidying up before the mad army chaplain comes to inspect our sleeping-bags.

3 I received a wound that will get me sent home when a mortar bomb, a mine and another mortar bomb landed in my dugout.

4 I am itching from all the lice in my shaggy fur coat and I wish I was back in my normal street clothes.

Sometimes the soldiers cheered themselves up by making fun of official army language. Their daily ration of spirits was 'service rum, diluted' – SRD. But the sergeant who served it out tended to get to a trench and say, 'I'll have mine with you,' and pour himself a tot.

He did the same in every trench. If you were unlucky enough to be in the last trench then there was no rum and a very drunk sergeant. So what did SRD stand for? 'Seldom reaches destination'!

And the Royal Army Medical Corps (RAMC) became the 'rob all my comrades' because soldiers suspected medical staff went through the pockets of the wounded men.

The same RAMC would sometimes be unsure what was wrong with a patient so they labelled him 'not yet diagnosed' (NYD). Soldiers swore the letters stood for 'not yet dead'.

Esses Ink Gee Nuts Ack London – Toc Ack London King!
No, that isn't a secret code to *disguise* the meaning of messages. It's a way of making messages quite *clear* over a crackling phone line. So 'Harry – Edward – London – London – Oranges' is 'Hello'.

Learn the list, impress your friends and confuse your teacher with the Great War code...

A = Ack	J = Johnnie	S = Esses
B = Beer	K = King	T = Toc
C = Charlie	L = London	U = Uncle
D = Don	M = Emma	V = Vic
E = Edward	N = Nuts	W = William
F = Freddie	O = Oranges	X = X-ray
G = Gee	P = Pip	Y = Yorker
H = Harry	Q = Queen	Z = Zebra
I = Ink	R = Robert	

Nutty names

Any names in the language of the enemy were suddenly unpopular.

France has a perfume called 'eau de Cologne' (water of Cologne), but Cologne is in Germany. They tried to change it to 'eau de Provence' because Provence is in France, but the idea never caught on.

The name changing went further in Germany. All bars, hotels and shops with English or French names were changed, causing great confusion.

In Breslau, the German military governor went to a sweet shop…

In 1915, Italy joined the war against Germany, and Berlin cafés stopped serving 'Italian salad'…

Jolly Germans

Even in the gloom of the war Germany kept its theatres open. But the plays were pretty miserable. The most popular one of 1917 was 'Maria Magdalena' about life in a small town. Well, that's not quite true … it's more about *death* in a small town!

Which character would you like to be? Can you pick the *two* that stayed alive?

1 Mrs Magdalena – a hard-working and caring mum
2 Mr Magdalena – a hard-working and caring dad
3 Maria – their daughter, a beautiful and popular girl
4 The cat – the family's faithful, furry friend
5 Fritz – Maria's lover
6 Hans – a rival for the love of Maria

Want a clue? Of the four who die, one dies in a duel, one suffers a fit on stage, one puts a bullet through their brain and (best of all) one throws themself down a well.

Answer: The mother dies of a fit on stage, Fritz is killed in a duel with Hans who commits suicide, so Maria jumps into a well. At the end only the father and the family cat are still alive!

Ropey rhymes

Poetry from the First World War is still remembered and enjoyed today by millions of people. Quite rightly.

But there were also some popular rhymes that have been forgotten. The simple poems and songs that soldiers repeated to try and stay cheerful in the bad times. The *bad* news is that most of them are too rude to be printed – even in a horrible history!

But here are a few that you may enjoy.

(Hint: Dig a hole in your back garden, flood it with water and sit there for a few hours while your family throw pots, pans or pianos out of upstairs windows on to you. This will get you in the mood.)

1 This limerick was popular around 1915…

There was a young lady of Ypres
Who was hit in the cheek by two snipers.
The tunes that she played
Through the holes that they made
Beat the Argyll and Sutherland pipers.

2 Private Stanley Woodburn wrote his will on a postcard and carried it in his pocket. He wrote it as a poem…

My belongings I leave to my next of kin,
My purse is empty there's nothing in;
My uniform, rifle, my pack and kit,
I leave to the poor devil they will fit;
But if this war I manage to clear
I'll keep it myself for a souvenir.

Private Woodburn was killed in France in April 1918.

3 Star of silent films, Charlie Chaplin, left his home in

England in 1913. When the war started a year later he did not return to join the army. Soldiers made up a popular song…

The moon shines bright on Charlie Chaplin,
His boots are cracking, for want of blacking.
And his little baggy trousers they want mending,
Before we send him to the Dardanelles…

Charlie didn't see the joke! 'I really thought they were coming to get me!' he said. 'It scared the daylights out of me.'

4 Many Brit soldiers had their own monthly magazines in the trenches. The poems they published were a bit of fun in the misery of the war…

There was a young Boche at Bazentin
Who liked the first trench that he went in.
But a 15 inch 'dud'
Sent him flat in the mud
And he found that his helmet was bent in.

5 Not all of the poems were funny. There were some things that soldiers said over and over again to cheer themselves up. This simple poem in a trenches' magazine took three of the sayings as its first three lines, then added its own fourth line…

It's a long road that has no turning,
It's never too late to mend;
The darkest hour is before the dawn
And even this war must end.

6 Poems were used in the hate-war against the enemy. In a children's magazine there was one to warn of the dangers of German toys which, of course, were supposed to be poisonous!

Little girls and little boys,
Never suck your German toys;
German soldiers licked will make
Darling Baby's tummy ache.
Parents, you should always try
Only British toys to buy;
Though to pieces they be picked,
British soldiers can't be licked.

7 Soldiers were fond of singing. When they couldn't find a suitable song they took a popular one and changed the words. In 1914 they were singing...

Though your heart may ache a while
*   ... never mind.*
Though your face may lose its smile
*   ... never mind.*
For there's sunshine after rain
And then gladness follows pain,
You'll be happy once again
*   ... never mind.*

The words were soon replaced by more bitter ones...

If you're hung up on barbed wire
*   ... never mind.*

Or…

> *If your sleeping place is damp*
>   *… never mind.*
> *If you wake up with a cramp*
>   *… never mind.*
> *If your trench should fall in some*
> *Fill your ears and make you dumb*
> *While the sergeant drinks your rum*
>   *… never mind.*

8 Love songs became war songs…

> *If you were the only girl in the world,*
> *And I were the only boy,*
> *Nothing else would matter in the world today,*
> *We would go on loving in the same old way.*
> *A garden of Eden, just made for two…*

Became…

> *If you were the only Boche in the trench,*
> *And I had the only bomb,*
> *Nothing else would matter in the world that day,*
> *I would blow you up into eternity.*
> *A Chamber of Horrors, just made for two…*

9 Even religious songs were made fun of. *What a Friend we Have in Jesus* became…

> *When this lousy war is over, oh how happy I will be,*
> *When I get my civvy clothes on, no more soldiering*
>   *for me.*
> *No more church parades on Sunday,*
> *No more putting in for leave.*
> *I will kiss the sergeant major,*
> *How I'll miss him, how I'll grieve.*

(The word 'lousy' in the first line was often replaced by a ruder word.)

10 But the song that summed up the First World War the best was the simplest one of all. It was sung to the tune of *Auld Lang Syne* (the one drunken parents join hands to sing at New Year and embarrass you with).

> *We're here because we're here because*
> *We're here because we're here.*
> *We're here because we're here because*
> *We're here because we're here.*

Says it all really.

Horrible historical joke
The soldiers in the front line enjoyed a joke, even in the terror of the trenches. They produced their own magazines and their jokes were often about the senior officers who were miles behind the lines when the shooting started.

One popular cartoon was this one…

Major-General (addressing the men before practising an attack in the training camp behind the lines). 'I WANT YOU TO UNDERSTAND THAT THERE IS A DIFFERENCE BETWEEN A REHEARSAL AND THE REAL THING. THERE ARE THREE ESSENTIAL DIFFERENCES. FIRST, THE ABSENCE OF THE ENEMY. NOW (turning to the Sergeant Major), WHAT IS THE SECOND DIFFERENCE?
Sergeant Major. 'THE ABSENCE OF THE GENERAL, SIR.'

Painful punishments

An army, like a school, needs discipline. Men have to learn to obey orders or else. Or else what? There were various punishments that your teachers might like to adopt for your school ... so keep this page out of their sight.

Field punishment No.1

In this notorious Brit punishment, the offender is lashed, or crucified, to a gun wheel, tied by wrists and ankles for one hour in the morning and one in the evening for up to 21 days. The intention is to humiliate the soldier. It was rumoured that soldiers were lashed to guns in action.

Toothbrush torture

The Germans had their own way of dealing with problem soldiers. Troublemakers in training were…

- made to scrub out the Corporals' room with a toothbrush.
- made to clear the barrack square of snow with hand-brushes and dustpans.

On Sundays (the recruits' only day off) they could be…

- forced to parade in full uniform with pack and rifle and then practise attacking and lying down in a muddy field until exhausted and filthy…
- …then, four hours later, made to report with every item of uniform and kit cleaned, hands bleeding and raw from the cleaning.

Once those trained men were sent to the front they were given a bunch of flowers to wear in their belts.

False fable

Many British soldiers believed that German soldiers were tied to their machine-guns to stop them from running away. In fact, German machine-gunners wore special belts with which they could carry their machine-guns and leave their hands free. If these soldiers were killed whilst carrying their gun, British soldiers would find the bodies 'tied' to the guns.

Cruel court martials

If a soldier was accused of a serious crime – like dropping his weapon and running away, or shooting himself in the foot to avoid going into battle – he'd be given a trial, known in the army as a 'court martial'.

Could you be a judge? Try these cases…

The case of Bellwarde Ridge

Private Allen and Private Burden were in the same regiment.

In June 1915 their regiment was ordered to move forward to the Bellwarde Ridge, France, which the Germans were defending furiously. Private Peter Allen didn't fancy walking towards machine-guns, so he took his rifle and shot himself in the leg. He was sent to hospital to recover and then ordered to serve two years in prison with hard labour.

Private Herbert Burden had joined up the year before. He told the recruiting officer he was 18 but he lied. He was just 16. When he was ordered to attack Bellwarde Ridge he was just 17 – the age of many schoolboys today. The attack was a disaster and Herbert's friends died all around him. He had done his best but, in the end he turned and ran from the battlefield.

He was court-martialled and found guilty. What would you do with Herbert? Remember what had happened to Peter Allen – who didn't even get to the fight. Remember that Herbert was only a boy. And remember that he'd been under heavy fire.

a) Give him a short rest then send him back into battle.
b) Send him home because he had been too young when he joined the army.
c) Give him two years' hard labour, the same as soldiers who wounded themselves.
d) Shoot him.

The case of king's crater
Sergeant Joe Tose and his officer, Lieutenant Mundy, left the safety of their trench to patrol a huge bomb crater in no man's land known as king's crater.

As they reached the crater they were attacked by a larger patrol of German soldiers. Lieutenant Mundy was shot.

Sergeant Tose ran back to the trench and decided to warn the rest of his battalion. To slow down the German attackers he jammed his rifle across the trench and set off for the rear trenches. As he had no weapon he was charged with 'casting away his weapon in the face of the enemy'.

Everyone said that he was a good soldier. (One witness said that the Germans spoke good English and, to add to the confusion, had called out 'Retreat!') What would you do with Joseph Tose?

a) Give him a medal for his quick thinking in saving his patrol.

b) Take his sergeant's position from him and send him back to fight as a private.

c) Strap him to a gun carriage for two hours a day for 21 days as Field Punishment No. 1.

d) Shoot him.

Answers: In both cases the men were shot. Men who avoided battle by shooting themselves were not executed. Herbert Burden was one of three 17-year-olds who were shot by the British in the First World War.

Sergeant Tose was disgraced and forgotten. He did not even get his name on his village war memorial until his case was looked at 80 years later. His name was finally added in 1997.

In the First World War the British shot 268 men for deserting their posts. (These are just two examples.) The German records were destroyed but they must have had the same problems. Yet it seems they shot only 48 of their own men. The Russians gave up shooting their own soldiers and the Australians never shot one.

1918 – The year of exhaustion

The Allies and the Central Powers have been battering at one another's doors for over three years and are exhausted. The Germans have decided to have one huge attack before they starve to death.

It is like charging with a battering-ram at a rotten door. The Allies give way and are pushed back, and back and back. The Germans seem to be the winners!

But the Germans are rushing forward too quickly. Their supplies can't keep up with them and they soon run out. When the Allies stop and turn, the Germans have nothing left to give. The Allies push on and on and on. All the way to Germany. The starved and feeble Germans are the losers … and all because they had been the winners.

Timeline 1918

January Britain is forced to have two meatless days a week and no meat for breakfast. Shops with margarine are raided by desperate women!

25 February Meat, butter and margarine rationed in the south of England and the queues (and the fighting shoppers) stop.

21 March Called the 'last day of trench warfare'. The Germans break out and smash the Allies back from the trenches. Shells fall on Paris.

1 April The Royal Air Force is formed and celebrate by shooting down German ace von Richthofen – the Red Baron – three weeks later.

May The German government wants young people to marry before they are 20 to produce more children for the country (which is running short of people).

June Thirty people die in Lancashire. They had Spanish 'flu. No one has any idea how many millions it's about to kill. Far more than the war, for sure.

18 July At the Marne River the Allies stop retreating. The tide is turning back towards Germany. The Russians massacre their royal family.

8 August German General Ludendorff calls this 'the black day for the German army' as they are driven back. Still, no one expects the war to end this year.

29 September Bulgarians have had enough and ask for peace. The beginning of the end for the Central Powers.

October German sailors are ordered to make one great last voyage to destroy the Brit fleet – or be destroyed. Sailors refuse and pour water on their ships' boiler fires.

9 November Kaiser Wilhelm is thrown out of Germany. He retires to Belgium. After what he did to them four years ago it's not

93

surprising they don't want him! He ends up in Holland.

11 November Armistice Day and peace is agreed at last. The peace document is signed at the 11th hour of this 11th day of the 11th month.

28 December Women vote in Britain for the first time. War has changed something, anyway.

Suffering shock

The huge shells that exploded during a battle killed and wounded millions of soldiers. But they had another effect that no one saw and few people understood in 1914–18. It was the effect of days of endless noise and dreadful fear on men's minds. Bombardments broke the minds of some men as surely as they broke the bodies of others.

The popular name for the effect was 'shell-shock' – the medical name is now 'post-traumatic stress disorder'. It doesn't matter what you call it really. Men suffered nightmares and fear of loud noises for the rest of their lives. It affected soldiers of all countries, during battles and long after them. Three survivors tell their stories…

In 1916, British Lieutenant Frederick Rees explained how shell-shock ruined a soldier's common sense…

Last night a man had an attack of nerves. He picked up a box of bombs, climbed out of the trench and threw them about in no man's land. He was lucky not to be shot. Either side would have shot him if he had come near when he still had those bombs. However, they got him back safe, poor chap.

George Bucher, a German officer in 1917, explained how the illness affected his side too. And some weren't as lucky as the man that Rees saw...

> *After four days of the bombardment a very young soldier had had enough. He climbed out of the trench with two hand-grenades from which he had taken the safety pins. He told his comrades what he thought about the war. He was going to run towards the British rifle fire and throw his grenades at them. He threatened to throw them at his comrades if they tried to stop him. They let him go...*

Lieutenant A G May, British Army, 1917, saw how shell-shock could affect different men in different ways...

> *The noise was impossible. Shells were bursting overhead. Near our front trench I saw a couple of our lads who had gone completely goofy. It was pitiful. One of them welcomed me like a long-lost friend and asked me to give him his baby. I picked up a tin hat from the ground and gave it to him. He cradled the hat as if it were a child, smiling and laughing without a care in the world, even though shells were falling all around us. I have no idea what happened to the poor chap but if he stayed there very long he must have been killed. A few days later I started to have uncontrollable jerking and shaking of my legs. I was quite upset because I was unable to stop it. The doctor told me I had shell-shock but I did not believe this. Later I was told to go to a special hospital for shell-shock victims.*

And, when the war had finished the nightmare of shell-shock went on and on, as a French soldier explained…

> *The noise of a slamming gate, a flaring gaslight, a train whistle, the barking of a dog or some boyish prank is enough to set off my trembling. Or, sometimes the trembling comes on without a reason. I went to a shop to do an errand for my wife. The crowd, the rustling silks, the colour of the goods – everything was a delight to look on after the misery of the trenches. I was happy and chatted merrily like a schoolboy on holiday. All of a sudden I felt my strength was leaving me. I stopped talking. I felt a shiver in my back, I felt my cheeks going hollow. I began to stare and the trembling came on again.*
>
> *In the tram I feel that people are looking at me and that gives me a terrible feeling. I feel they are looking at me with pity. Some excellent woman offers me her seat. I am deeply touched; but they look at me and say nothing; what are they thinking of me?*

'They look at me and say nothing.' That was part of the pain. No one knew how to deal with a shell–shocked man.

No one knew *what* to say.

Cruel for creatures

The animals that went to war didn't start the fight and didn't ask to go. But they were shot at and bombed and gassed and diseased as cruelly as their human masters. It was beastly being a beast in the First World War. If you're the sort of person who's pained by the thought of a pet with a prick in its paw, it may be better to skip this section. If you enjoy raw hamster-burgers at school dinners, read on...

Creature cwiz

True or false?

1 In the First World War, British dogs were horses.

2 The best horses were saved for the Army priests (the chaplains).

3 German soldiers wiped out a herd of rare European bison in Poland.

4 A British regiment made a miniature steel helmet for their pet dog.

5 The German Army fitted their horses with gas masks.

6 A chick named Dick was used to detect enemy aircraft.

7 Goldfish were banned from the battle areas because water was precious.

OI! STOP THAT. WATER DOESN'T GROW ON TREES YOU KNOW

GULP

8 Horse droppings were used to make gas for heat and light.

9 Soldiers kept canaries because their song cheered everyone up.

10 The Allies won the war because they had a better supply of horses.

Answers:

1 True. The British Army supplied all the animals they needed but, to keep everything simple, they called these animals 'horses' … even if they were guard dogs, oxen, reindeer or camels!

2 False. The chaplains were given horses at the start of the war but there was a shortage of horses for the fighting men. The chaplains had their horses taken from them and were given bicycles instead!

3 False. The herd of bison wiped out the Germans! The animals were grazing peacefully and ignoring the soldiers. Then a rifle was fired and the angry bison charged. They gored and trampled the German soldiers to death. Only 20 soldiers survived.

4 True. The dog was a stray that adopted the gunners. It became their lucky mascot. The death of the dog would have meant bad luck, so they protected it from 'stray' bullets and shells with a steel helmet.

5 True. The masks (which looked a bit like a nose-bag) didn't work very well and didn't protect the animals' eyes from the stinging gas. But at least the kindly Germans were *trying* to help their four-legged friends.

6 True. Driver David Spink rescued a half-starved chicken near St Quentin in 1918 and christened it Dick. When Allied aircraft flew over it was fine, but it dived for cover (and so did David Spink's company) when an enemy aircraft was overhead. After the war Dick travelled back to Britain in Driver Spink's haversack and enjoyed a happy retirement.

7 False. Goldfish were very useful. After a gas attack the gas helmets were rinsed with water. A goldfish was then dropped into the rinsing water. If the goldfish died then the mask was still poisoned and needed to be washed again. (Sadly, there is no record of a goldfish ever getting a medal for bravery.)

8 True. A horse produced about 14 or 15 kilograms of droppings every day. (Do you ever wonder who gets the job of measuring these things?) The British alone had 870,000 horses in action by the end of the war. That is nearly 13 million kilos of horse muck being produced *every day*! Some was buried, some burned, some spread on fields as fertilizer. But some was heated to give off a gas that powered lamps and heaters. (Might it have been quicker just to put a lighted match to the horse's bum?)

9 False. Soldiers *did* keep canaries, but they were used in underground tunnels to check for gas. (If the bird fell off its perch then there was gas down there.) Some of the bird handlers became very attached to their canaries and risked their own lives to save the birds during gas attacks. Why bother? They could always find another canary going cheap... Cheep! Cheep!

10 True. At least that's what British General Haig said after the war. 'If the Germans had a horse service as good as the British then they would have won the war.'

Brave beasts

Men and women performed some incredibly brave acts in the face of the enemy. A German hero was covered in Iron Crosses, a British hero was covered in medals and an American hero, called Cher Ami, was covered in feathers. Because Cher Ami was a pigeon!

Duck, dove!
No, Cher Ami didn't fly over enemy forces and drop bombs on them, stupid. He carried a message from US soldiers in battle and saved dozens of lives. Imagine the sadness when he finally died...

DOVE CONQUERS ALL

Cher Ami is dead. The pigeon that won the hearts of all true Americans, has hopped the twig and passed peacefully away to that great pigeon loft in the sky.

It was just a year ago that Cher Ami flew to fame when he joined Major Charles Whittlesey's brigade. In the Argonne Forest, eastern France, the brigade found itself surrounded by enemy forces, starving and exhausted with many dead and wounded. Then shells began to land on the American survivors – but they were American shells aimed at them by mistake. There was only one way to get a message out of the deadly circle of machine-guns: a carrier pigeon.

Whittlesey scribbled a note: 'Our own forces are dropping shells on us! For heaven's sake stop it!' He took a pigeon from its basket but the frightened bird broke loose and flew for home – the US army base camp. There was just one bird left – one last hope – a black cock called Cher Ami. Whittlesey clipped the message to the brave bird's leg and set it free. But Cher Ami flew up to the nearest tree and began preening its feathers. The brigade threw sticks and stones but still the perverse pigeon refused to budge. Finally Whittlesey climbed the tree and shook the branch. Cher Ami took the hint and set off for home.

The enemy saw at once that it was carrying a message and turned the full firepower of the forces towards it. One shot took off part of the battered bird's leg, passed through its chest and knocked out one eye. The peppered pigeon lost height, then, amazingly, recovered and flew on to deliver the message and the brigade was saved. 'Without that bird we'd have been wiped out, that is certain,' Whittlesey said. 'The 384 men who survived owed their lives to Cher Ami's courage.'

The heroic homing pigeon was patched up and brought back to a hero's welcome in America, where he died peacefully yesterday. He will be stuffed and go on display at the Smithsonian Institute.

Feathered fighters

1 Gallant pigeons like Cher Ami had another use. If soldiers became cut off from their supplies and were starving they could always eat the birds!

2 Pigeon *pies* are very tasty, but pigeon *spies* were also valuable. Baskets full of British pigeons were dropped into

French and Belgian villages that had been captured by the Germans. Villagers could then attach messages to the pigeons who would fly back to Britain. The messages could tell the Allies what the enemy was up to. This is spying, of course, and the punishment for spying in war was to be shot. But it was even more dangerous being a pigeon. Sixteen thousand were dropped but only one in ten returned.

3 The Germans took the problem of pigeon spies seriously. They cleverly planted baskets of German pigeons in the villages. Anyone who attached a message would see the bird fly off to Germany.

4 The Germans also formed squadrons of hawks and falcons to catch any pigeon flying over the English Channel back to Britain. This was rotten luck if you were an innocent pigeon on a day trip to Paris.

EEK!

5 In the mud and rain of 1917 a group of soldiers were cut off and attached a message to a pigeon. The pigeon was too soaked to fly. It flopped into no man's land ... then started walking towards the German lines with its message! If the Germans knew the Brits were alone they would have

attacked and finished them off! The Brits had to shoot the plodding pigeon. Their other bird was just as wet. One soldier suggested drying it in the dugout oven, but in the end the soldiers dried it by blowing on its feathers. It worked.

6 A French pigeon saved hundreds of troops at Verdun in 1916. The French were being shelled by Germans but had no heavy guns of their own to fight back. They wanted to get a message out to their gunners to say, 'Here are the German gun positions. Aim at them and stop them destroying us.' A greyhound got the message through, though he was wounded. And a pigeon got through just before it died of its wounds. The pigeon was given France's highest *human* medal for bravery – the *Legion d'Honneur*. The men and women who won the *Legion d'Honneur* must have been a bit annoyed by this! It's like saying, 'Here's your medal. Wear it with pride. You are as brave as a pigeon!'

The tale of a dog
Pigeons weren't the only courageous creatures to help their human masters in the First World War. There were dog heroes too. Heroes like Stubby the American pit bull terrier…

Stubby was a poor and homeless stray when Rob Conroy found him on the streets of Hartford, Connecticut. Nothing could separate these pals, not even the First World War. When Rob went to war, Stubby went with him.

Stubby was smuggled all the way to the war zone with the gallant guys in the 102nd Infantry Battalion. But he was no pampered pet, oh no! Stubby was a priceless guard dog with sharper eyes and ears than any sentry.

No matter what the enemy threw at him, Stubby ran out on to the battlefield and found the wounded. Then he lay beside them till the stretchers reached him. They called it no man's land, but it wasn't no dog's land!

And while the tired troopers slept, Stubby watched over them. One night he warned them of a gas attack. Another night a sneaking enemy soldier slipped into the US trenches – and left with Stubby's teeth in his butt!

Stubby fought in 17 battles. There was no way they could pin all his medals on his brave little breast – so they had a special blanket made. When the proud pooch met President Woodrow Wilson he wore it.

The First World War ended, but Stubby's work went on. He toured the country with Rob Conroy to raise money for victims of the fighting. What a courageous canine! Stubby! Man's best friend ... ever!

Daring dogs

1 Dogs made useful messengers. They could be trained to run over the battlefield with messages fastened to their collars. Enemy soldiers watched for messenger dogs and tried to turn them into dead dogs.

2 Of course the Germans had dogs just as brave as Stubby. One was used to carry secret messages backwards and forwards across the trenches. The German dog was the perfect spy courier. The British tried everything to capture him – nets and traps all failed – until the Allied soldiers came up with a devious dodge. They set a female dog to attract him into their hands. One wag of her tail and the German spy-dog was caught. (Let this be a lesson to you gentlemen readers ... if a young lady wags her tail at you then *paws* before you run after her!)

3 Dogs were also put in harnesses and used to drag machine-guns around the battlefield. The Italian army used them to pull supply carts over the Alps. In the summer this would have turned them into 'hot dogs', I guess.

4 Dogs also had reels of telephone cable strapped to their backs. As they ran along they left a trail of cable behind them and linked the men in the trenches to the support troops behind them. Enemy gunners were always trying to cut these links and would shoot at cable layers. Dogs were faster than men, smaller and harder to hit than men, and it didn't matter so much if a dog was killed ... unless you were the dog, of course.

5 When the war started, German shepherd dogs in Britain suddenly became unpopular – just because of their name! So the name was changed to 'Alsatian' and it's stayed that way ever since. (If you want to test your teacher, tell them of the German shepherd name change then say, 'What *other* creatures changed their English name in the First World War?' The answer is ... the British Royal Family. They changed their family name from the German Saxe-Coburg-Gotha to Windsor. Like the Alsatians they too are stuck with it.)

107

6 Some dogs went across to the enemy! No, they weren't traitors. Early in the war French and German troops were in trenches just 30 metres apart. They sent each other friendly messages, newspapers and tobacco, tied to the dog's collar. One French corporal had left his wife behind in Germany when the war started. A dog brought him a message from her saying she was quite well and sent her love; the Germans passed it on by puppy post.

7 Terriers were useful for killing rats in the trenches. A devoted soldier wrote a poem to his dog, Jim…

Jim

A tough little, rough little beggar,
And merry the eyes on him.
But no German or Turk
Can do dirtier work
With an enemy rat than Jim.

And when the light's done and night's falling,
And shadows are darkling and dim,
In my coat you will nuzzle
Your pink little muzzle
And growl in your dreams, little Jim.

There is no record of what the rats thought of little Jim.

Of course not every company in the trenches had a rat-catcher like Jim. What did these poor soldiers do? They tamed the rats and kept them as pets instead!

Rotten for rats

Rats enjoyed the First World War … mostly. There was always plenty to eat because the soldiers brought tons of supplies with them. But most soldiers hated the robbing rodents and spent a lot of their spare time trying to massacre the creepy creatures. Apart from shooting them in the open they also tried some sneaky tricks. The following were all tried in the trenches with great success…

Vanquish Vile Vermin!

Method 1

1 If rats have been at your bread then place the ruined loaves on the floor of your dugout.

2 Find yourself a spade and torches. Switch out the lights.

3 When you hear the rats swarming over the bread then switch on the torches and smash the rats to a pulp.

Method 2

1 Place cordite at the entrance to rat holes and light it. The smoke will drive out the rats.

2 Wait by the exit and smash them with wooden clubs.

 Method 3

1 Put a bayonet on the end of your rifle.

2 Put a piece of cheese on the end of the bayonet.

 Point it towards the enemy lines.

3 When a rat begins to nibble at the cheese, pull the trigger. You can't miss!

Horrible Histories health warning: Cordite was used as an explosive to propel shells from guns. A group of Australian soldiers smoked out rats this way until the cordite came in contact with an unexploded German mine. Twenty men were injured ... but the rats were probably pulped!

Soldiers believed that rats knew when a bombardment was coming because the creatures would run away from the trenches that were in danger. They even believed that the biggest rats – usually nicknamed 'corpse rats' – could kill a cat or a dog.

German soldiers often kept cats in the front line, not simply to catch rats but because cats also gave early warning of a British gas attack. They became restless as though they could detect the poison gas in very low concentrations before the main cloud appeared.

Horrible historical joke

In June 1917 it was against British law to feed pigeons. This was part of the plan to save food. Not everyone agreed that this was a smart move.

In one of the soldiers' magazines the following joke appeared...

> *A driver has been punished for giving his bread ration to his horse. He certainly deserved it. We are totally against cruelty to animals.*

Women and children

The First World War affected women and children more than any other war had done. Before 1914 wars had been about men fighting men; women and children had been simply victims – they got themselves massacred if they were unlucky enough to be in a battle zone. They were starved, lost husbands and children, but they didn't *give* a lot to war efforts. That was about to change.

Wicked women

In July 1915, 30,000 women paraded in London under the banner, 'We demand the right to serve'. Women slowly began to take up jobs in war-work, especially making weapons and ammunition (munitions).

The miserable men didn't want women in the factories. They thought it would give the women a taste of freedom and change them. They were right! By the end of the war

British women could…
- smoke cigarettes openly
- drink in public houses
- openly use cosmetics
- swear
- wear short skirts and bras
- wear short hair (to control the nits)
- go to the cinemas without a man
- play football (most factories started girl teams)
- Then, Land Girls, who'd taken the jobs of farm labourers, began to wear their trousers off duty!

In short, they started doing all the things men had been doing for years. (Oh, all right, you *didn't* see a lot of men in lipstick, short skirts and bras, but you know what I mean!) And women still do these shocking things today!

The German women worked just as hard but didn't earn the same sort of freedom. German men did not approve of freedom for their women. In 1917 a German politician, claimed that…

Female freedom in England has destroyed all family life there. The women are so bad that more married men than single men offered themselves as recruits for the Army. The married men, in fact, join up to escape from their wives.

112

In one or two cases he may have been right!

French women were allowed to drink but only very weak wine.

If it sounds fun to be a British woman, then the working women paid a high price. They worked in dangerous war jobs where…

- 81 died in accidents
- 71 female workers died in explosions
- 61 died of poisoning

…and they were only paid half of a man's wages.

It's a fair cop
How did they get poisoned? By working with high explosives like TNT that got into their lungs and blood. The symptoms were...

- First your nose hurt, then it bled, your eyes stung and your throat became sore.

- You would get pains in the chest and stomach, diarrhoea and skin rashes.

- If you weren't treated, you'd get sickness, giddiness,

swollen hands and feet, drowsiness and finally death.

But this didn't stop the women taking risks with the TNT. In September 1917, a young munitions worker was fined for stealing TNT from the factory where she worked. She stole it because it was common for workers to use TNT powder to give their hair a chestnut colour. But a red-head could become red-hot if you struck a match near her hair!

Britain created its first policewomen during the First World War and one of their duties was to stop women workers taking explosives out of the factories, and to stop them taking cigarettes or matches into the factories. Policewoman Greta East kept a diary of her life on duty at a South Wales Munitions factory…

10 April 1917

The girls here are troublesome about bringing in cigarettes and matches. Last week a woman came to the Women Police

Office and asked me to rescue her coat from the cloakroom as she had a train to catch. She said I'd recognize the coat because it had her payslip in the pocket. But, when I searched the pockets I found them full of cigarettes. Of course the poor wretch had to be prosecuted and fined. She must have forgotten about them.

A pretty dim worker, but not so dim as the underground toilets they had to use. Greta went on to describe the conditions…

There are no drains because the ground is below sea level. The result is the toilets are a horrible and smelly swamp. There were no lights in the lavatories and those same lavatories are often full of rats and very dirty. The girls are afraid to go in.

With no lights how did you find the toilet paper? Or how did you avoid reaching out for toilet paper and picking up a rat by mistake? Yeuch!

By the end of war, 30 police forces had appointed women – another First World War idea that is still with us. (Though some, like Manchester, refused.)

Warring women

Not all women were happy to 'serve' by making shells. In September 1914, French newspapers reported the story of a 28-year-old laundry woman who had been discovered fighting at the front in the uniform of a French soldier. She was sent back to her old job at the laundry but protested angrily. (Just like most people, she probably hated all the ironing.)

There is a story that a British woman also got as far as the trenches, dressed in the kilts of a Highland soldier. (This was very suitable because the Germans called the Highlanders 'ladies from Hell'.) She did it for a bet but was caught and returned to Britain. (It was probably the handbag that gave her away.)

By 1917 the Russian Army was so weak it created a women's battalion, 'The Battalion of Death', to help. Three hundred women were led by the incredible Maria Botchkareva. Maria had been married at 15 and suffered terribly at the hands of two brutal husbands. War was wonderful compared to what she endured at home! She suffered frostbite and several wounds but survived. (She probably volunteered for the pleasure of being able to shoot at men!)

Battling babes

There are many stories of boys going into army recruiting

offices to join up even though they were under age. Many army recruiting officers were willing to let them join anyway. Of course it was their duty to check on the age and reject the ones who *said* they were under age. This story is true and happened hundreds of times all over the world...

Parents were able to 'claim out' their sons if they could trace them, and the boy soldiers were sent home.

- Myer Rosenblum from London joined the London Welsh Regiment in August 1914, aged 13 years and nine months, but was 'claimed out' by his father in October 1914. He joined up again and was sent to Gallipoli where he was wounded in June 1915. His father claimed him again when he was sent back to England.

- Private James Bartaby joined the 7th East Surreys, as a volunteer, on 20 January 1915, aged 13 years and ten months. After training, he went to France in late May and was wounded and sent home in October 1915.

- In October 1915, Arthur Peyman – 'described as 19 years of age' – was in court, charged with being absent from his regiment since the end of August. During the case, his mother appeared and produced his birth certificate, showing that he was only 14 years old.

At least Arthur Peyman escaped being shot for leaving his regiment. Other boys were not so lucky.

Trench tot

It wasn't just the fighting boys who ended up in the trenches. Sometimes small children were caught up in the battlefields. In early 1916, Philip Impey was going back into the trenches near La Basse, when he found a small girl abandoned in a ditch. He couldn't take her to safety and he couldn't leave her, so Philip picked her up and carried her into the trenches.

During the week, she climbed on to the parapet in full view of the Germans, who were close by. German soldiers shouted to her, offering her sweets and chocolate.

When the soldiers left the front, they took her with them. She was eventually sent to England and survived. Sadly, Philip Impey was killed in action soon after.

Cheeky Charlies

British kids in 1917 were getting out of control. There was a huge increase in vandalism, theft and street crimes among school-aged children.

- Some people blamed the fact that their fathers were away in the army.
- Others blamed the cinema. (Nowadays they'd blame the television, so nothing much changes, does it?)
- A third excuse was weak teachers – old ladies, brought out of retirement, to take the place of the men who had gone off to fight. (Imagine that! Kids taking advantage of their tough teacher being away. You wouldn't do a thing like that, would you?)

In Germany the children had a surprise when the war started. In Berlin all English teachers were sacked! (But that was wartime so don't raise your hopes that it may happen for you!)

But by 1917 German children were so hungry they had a desperate new game ... stealing any food they could find.

Wrinklies at war

- The oldest French soldier was 78 years old.
- Italy's oldest soldier was 74.
- Lieutenant Henry Webber was, at 67, the oldest British soldier killed in action at the Somme in July 1916.
- In December 1915, James White of Sowerby Bridge was sent home from the trenches when it was discovered that he had fought the Zulu War of 1878, and was 70 years old.
- In June 1918, the *Yorkshire Evening Press* told the story of a merchant sailor, William Jessop of Hull. He was 72 years old and had been torpedoed seven times.

William said...

- In 1915, Chief Gunner Israel Harding had his left leg broken when his ship was blown up in the Dardanelles, near Turkey. He was 84 years old. He had once been a trawlerman but had run away to join the Royal Navy and first saw active service in the Crimean War of 1853–56.

Frightful 'flu facts

By November 1918 the war had killed about eight-and-a-half million people. But that was nothing to what happened next. Spanish 'flu spread around the world...

- People collapsed in the streets, at work and at home.
- It appeared to hit young, healthy people more than the old or very young.
- The deadly virus attacked the lungs, which hardened, making breathing impossible: the victim finally drowned in their own fluid.
- At the moment of death, virus-laden fluid poured out the victim's mouth and nose.
- By May 1919 Spanish 'flu had killed over 200,000 in the UK and 20 million around the world – far more in one year than the war had managed in four.
- It killed more people than the Black Death.
- No one knew where it came from or why it suddenly went away.

Some men survived four years of shells, bullets and bombs only to get home safely ... and die of the 'flu!

IF I CAN LIVE THROUGH THAT, I CAN LIVE THROUGH ANYTH...
BAFF

Strange but true

US soldier, Major Harry S Truman, kept his battalion guns firing till the last seconds of the First World War.

Nearly 30 years later the Major was US President Harry S Truman. He ordered the dropping of atomic bombs on Japanese towns. This brought the Second World War to an end.

In a strange way you could say the same man fired the last shots in the *two* world wars.

Test your teacher

Try this quick quiz on your teacher and watch as they strain their brain cell to the limit. If they get a question wrong you can jeer because they're a dunce – if they get it right you can jeer because they're probably old enough to remember the First World War!

1 If you lived in Britain in 1916 and wanted to know what it was like in the trenches, you could visit some. Where?
a) On the French side of the Western Front near the town of Ypres.
b) Behind the German lines, near Berlin.
c) In Blackpool.

2 A British minister in charge of food production was called what?
a) The Controller of Potatoes.
b) The Fat Controller.
c) Director of Army Food Transportation (DAFT).

3 Soldiers had an average of 20 lice crawling over their bodies. But what was the record?
a) 428.
b) 1,428.
c) 10,428.

I DON'T KNOW WHAT'S WORSE, HAVING THEM OR HAVING TO COUNT THEM

4 French newspapers of 1914 had reports that their soldiers were very comfortable in the trenches with what?
a) Wine.

123

b) Women.

c) Central heating.

5 What was a 'wibble-wobble'?
a) A soldier's name for a fat general.
b) Another name for a tank.
c) A horse with an injured leg.

6 The women who worked with TNT explosive were nicknamed 'canaries'. Why?
a) They were so happy they sang like canaries while they worked.
b) The TNT caused their hair to turn canary yellow.
c) Because the factory owners were getting 'cheep' labour.

7 The First World War changed fashions and almost killed off one fashion. What?
a) Men wearing top hats to work.
b) Women wearing knickers.
c) Children wearing wooden clogs.

8 Kaiser Wilhelm of Germany was a powerful but crazy king. What was his hobby?

a) Pulling the wings off flies.

b) Throwing darts at pictures of his grandmother, Queen Victoria.

c) Chopping down trees.

9 Brit Patrick Gara was arrested for trying to dodge joining the army. His excuse was…

a) His mum wouldn't let him.

b) He was a coward and was afraid of getting hurt.

c) He didn't know there was a war on.

10 Brits with hard tennis courts were suspected by the police. Why?

a) Police believed they had been prepared as gun platforms for an invasion.

b) Tennis parties were a good cover for two spies to meet and swap messages hidden in tennis balls.

c) Police thought they were up to some secret racket.

Answers:

1c) That's right, Blackpool. Soldiers recovering from wounds built replicas of the trenches at Loos. (That was a battlefield on the Western Front, not a toilet.) German people could visit the same sort of thing in Berlin.

2a) Imagine being called the Controller of Potatoes! Think of all the jokers who'd write to you and say, 'My potatoes are very naughty. Can you control them for me?'

3c) As well as having 10,428 lice in his shirt there were about 10,253 lice eggs waiting to hatch. The same man would have had thousands more in his trousers, socks and hair. It's surprising he had any blood left after the lice had had their lunch!

MAN WITH LICE (OR LICE WITH MAN)

4c) The truth is the soldiers in the trenches had to be very careful about lighting fires. The smoke gave enemy gunners something to aim at. So you could light a fire and be shelled to death, or not light a fire and freeze to death!

5b) The army name for a tank was a 'landship', but they collected lots of other names too: Slug, Whale, Toad, Tortoise, Land-crab, Behemoth, Boojum. Newspapers couldn't give away the secret by showing pictures, so Brit writers described a 'long, low, dust-coloured tortoise' while French newspapers reported they were equipped in front with 'some kind of cow catcher'. But to most soldiers it looked like a water 'tank' and that name stuck.

6b) TNT caused nasty skin rashes and its fumes turned

the girls' hair bright mustard yellow – the colour of canaries. These unfortunate girls were often refused service in restaurants whose owners said, 'You are *unsightly*. Go away because you are putting the other customers off their food!'

7a) War changed British ways of life – posh people who would never have dreamed of travelling on a tram or bus before 1914, now travelled to work every day … paying their fares to 'conductorettes'. Women's fashion changed as a shortage of steel ended the wearing of tight corsets. City gents stopped wearing top hats as they were a nuisance on a bus or underground train with a low roof.

8c) Willy enjoyed felling trees at his palace at Potsdam. He was mad about stripping off the bark – which proves he was barking mad.

9b) In 1916, Patrick Gara was up before magistrates in Selby, Yorkshire, for avoiding military service. He was asked why he had not joined the army. He replied that he thought that he was safer in Selby than in the trenches! He was fined £2 and escorted to the nearest barracks. A year later, a man called Graham Whitlaw was up before the magistrates in London for not reporting for military service. His excuse was that he was a duke and a bishop and he had been appointed Chief of the Army. He'd been appointed by King George IV (who had been dead almost 100 years). Of course Whitlaw was trying to act as if he was too mad to serve. It didn't work.

10a) Daft, but true. What use would a gun platform be in someone's back garden? You could always shell your neighbour's peas, I suppose.

Epilogue

There were lots of tragedies in the First World War. Almost every family in Britain, France, Germany and Russia lost someone. You can go to any town or village and see the names of the dead, carved on stone memorials. Many of the men who joined together died together and left their home towns desolate.

But that wasn't the *real* tragedy. The cruellest thing of all was that the First World War *didn't* solve any problems and it *didn't* bring peace. It led to the Second World War and far, far more misery, death and destruction.

Those whose names are carved on the memorials believed they were fighting for peace. Many would have given their lives gladly if they knew they had died in 'the war to end all wars'.

What went wrong? Big mistakes and small accidents. One accident so small that no one noticed it at the time. It happened in a German dugout during the Battle of the Somme. A British shell smashed into the trench and killed most of the Germans in it. But by a hideous chance one German escaped with just a shell splinter in his face.

He lived. He lived to start another war. His name was Adolf Hitler. Lucky Hitler – unlucky world.

Sometimes history is changed by great events like the First World War – sometimes it is changed by freak accidents in a fraction of a second: the arrow that hit King Harold in the eye at the Battle of Hastings ... the shell that *failed* to kill Hitler.

History can be horrible. But each of us should find our nearest war memorial, stand in front of it and read the names.

Then say, 'Never again.'

If everyone says that, and means it, then the deaths will not have been such a waste.

FRIGHTFUL
FIRST WORLD
WAR
GRISLY QUIZ

Now find out if you're a Frightful First World War expert!

BEASTLY BATTLES

There were lots of famous fights and crazy campaigns throughout the war. See if you can figure out which of these beastly battle facts are true and which are false.

1. The Battle of Mons began on 23 August 1914, one of the earliest big actions of the First World War. British soldiers later claimed they were protected during the battle by a group of angels. True or false?

2. French soldiers were taken to the front line for the Battle of the Marne in September 1914 by taxi. True or false?

3. There were three major battles around Ypres in Belgium throughout the war. In the last battle there a young Winston Churchill – the great Second World War leader – was almost blinded in a gas attack. True or false?

4. The Battle of the Somme began on 1 July 1916 and went on until 18 November. The French and British attacked German lines. In that time the British suffered 57,470 casualties. True or false?

5. The French and British attack at Arras began on 1 October 1914. It was a failure for the Allies because they only managed to capture a single hill. True or false?

6. Verdun was the longest battle of the war, beginning in February 1916. The Germans were led by a prince. True or false?

7. The Battle of Cambrai in November 1917 was such a disaster for the British that the government ordered that church bells were not allowed to ring. True or false?

8. The Battle of Jutland in 1916 was the most famous sea battle of the war. The British won and the German fleet did not sail again for the rest of the war. True or false?

9. The Battle of Neuve-Chapelle was fought between 10–13 March 1915. More shells were fired in the first 35 minutes of this battle than in the whole of the Boer War, just 15 years earlier. True or false?

10. The Battle of the Aisne began in September 1914. It was named after a nearby town. True or false?

TERRIBLE TRENCHES QUICK QUIZ

Take this quick quiz to find out if you would have survived life in the terrible trenches or been beaten by the Bosch.

1. Poisonous gas was used for the first time in the First World War. What would you do if you were caught in a gas attack in the trenches? (Clue: you might need a wee bit of help)

2. How could you tell when an enemy bombardment was about to begin? (Clue: vile vermin)

3. Trench toilets were buckets or holes dug into the mud. With hundreds of soldiers suffering from deadly dysentery, they filled up quickly. Where could you go to poo if the foul latrines were full? (Clue: a number two in no-man's land?)

4. Things could get pretty chilly in the trenches and lots of icy infantry soldiers suffered from frostbite. How did they save their frozen feet? (Clue: you'll get snow help from me!)

5. Trench foot was caused by cold, damp and unhealthy conditions (the trenches were filled with mud and water and poo and bodies). What could you do to prevent having your feet chopped off because of this disgusting disease? (Clue: grease is the word)

6. Lice loved life in the trenches. They would live on the soldiers and make a mighty meal of them. How did the men try to get rid of the lice? (Clue: flaming lice!)

7. Many soldiers tried to give themselves a 'blighty' (a wound just serious enough to be sent home) to escape the terrible trenches, but what would happen if they were found out? (Clue: it was a deathly disaster)

8. If you were sniper, what was the best way to avoid being seen by the enemy? (Clue: think about it – you'll soon twig)

9. In an emergency, what was the best way to make a splint for a soldier with broken bones? (Clue: you're gun-na have to think of something)

10. How did the army try to reduce cases of dysentery in the trenches, caused by dirty water? (Clue: water with a twist)

NUTTY NICKNAMES
Soldiers in the First World War had nicknames for everything – their weapons, ranks and rations. See if you can

understand the soldiers' slang and figure out which weird words mean what.

1. Tommy   a) Senior officers
2. Brass hats   b) Experienced soldier
3. Blighty   c) Britain
4. Coffin nails   d) Cigarettes
5. Jerry   e) British soldier
6. Old sweat   f) Jam
7. Whizz bang   g) German soldier
8. Conchie   h) Tea
9. Char   i) Conscientious objector
10. Pozzy   j) Artillery shell

ANSWERS

Beastly Battles

1. True. The British managed to beat back the Germans despite being outnumbered and they thought that God had sent a ghostly army of angels to help them. To this day no one really knows the truth about the Angels of Mons...

2. True. France ordered every taxi cab in Paris to be available to take soldiers to the frontline so they would get there in time for the big battle.

3. False. It was a young Adolf Hitler who was smothered by the ghastly gas. In the whole of the First World War horrid Hitler was awarded six medals for bravery!

4. False. The casualty figure of nearly 58,000 was for the first day alone – 1 July. This is still a record.

5. False. It was a success for the Allies because they managed to capture a single hill. That hill, known as Vimy Ridge, captured

by Canadian forces, was very important!

6. True. The Germans at the Battle of Verdun were led by Crown Prince William, son of crazy Kaiser William II.

7. False. The Battle of Cambrai was considered such a success for the British that church bells were allowed to be rung for the first time since the war began.

8. True (and false). It's true that the German fleet was so badly damaged by the British that it spent the rest of the war in dock, but no one could claim it was a great success for the British – they lost thousands of men.

9. True. Methods of warfare and weapons had changed dramatically between the end of the Boer War in 1902 and the First World War.

10. False. Like many other battles in the First World War, including the Somme and the Marne, it was named after a nearby river.

Terrible Trenches Quick Quiz

1. Pee on your hanky and then tie it over your nose and mouth. This weird wee trick really worked – the chemicals in urine kept out the gas.

2. Watch the rats. Rats were everywhere in the stinking trenches and soldiers believed that they knew instinctively when an attack was about to happen and disappeared. If you couldn't see a rotten rat then you were probably in for a beastly bombardment.

3. A shell-hole. Who needed specially dug holes when the Germans made them for you with their bombs? Just find a cosy shell hole and squat.

4. Rubbing them with snow. In fact we now know that rubbing frostbite with anything actually makes the damage worse. So

rubbing it with snow was not only parky and painful it was also pointless!

5. Cover your feet with grease made from whale oil. A single battalion in the trenches could use up to ten gallons of gooey grease every day!

6. They would burn them with a candle. This was a tricky business and more than one careless corporal set his clothes on fire in the process.

7. They would be shot. Yup – the usual punishment for soldiers who tried to cheat their way out of the war was to be sent for trial and killed.

8. Camouflage yourself as a tree. Sneaky snipers would slither into no-man's land to get closer to the enemy. To avoid being spotted they would hide under cover of a fake tree!

9. Use your rifle. Other things could be used to help soldiers with broken bones until the medics arrived – pieces of wood, bayonets, swords – but the rifle made a good sturdy splint. Not much good if you run into the enemy while your gun's tied to your lieutenant's leg, though!

10. They added chloride of lime. This was believed to purify the water supplied – but the soldiers hated it because it made the water taste disgusting!

Nutty Nicknames
1.e) 2.a) 3.c) 4.d) 5.g) 6.b) 7.j) 8.i) 9.h) 10.f)

INTERESTING INDEX

Where will you find 'beetle-racing', 'fried lice' and 'smelly whale oil' in an index? In a Horrible Histories book, of course!

138

WOEFUL
SECOND WORLD
WAR

Introduction

History can be horrible – but some times in history are more horrible than others...

JUST LIKE LESSONS – HISTORY LESSONS ARE MORE HORRIBLE THAN GAMES LESSONS!

Of course, this is all a matter of opinion...

IF YOU ASK ME GAMES LESSONS ARE MORE HORRIBLE THAN ANYTHING IN THE WORLD!

Most people seem to agree that wartimes are the *worst* of times. And wars in the twentieth century were the *most* horrible of all. Even the winners suffered terrible losses, and new weapons weren't fussy about who they exterminated – suffering schoolkids shot, peaceful pensioners pulverized and blameless babies bombed.

You might think it's easy to drop a bomb from an aeroplane because you don't have to see the suffering you cause. But war brings out the worst side of some human beings. The monsters. The few people who enjoy the pain and torture and death they are causing…

And it brings out the best in others – the ones who risk their own lives to fight for what they think is right. The heroes and heroines.

Most people are somewhere in between. Hopefully *you'll* never have to suffer in a war. But you will be tested from time to time. You may like to decide if you'd act like a monster or a heroine.

Any old boring history book will tell you about the battles and the dates and the facts and figures. But what you want to know is what it was really like to live through those days. How did people really behave in the Second World War? And how would you have behaved?

What you need is a horrible history of the Second World War! So read on…

Terrible timeline

11 November 1918 End of First World War. Germany battered and bitter. They blame their leaders, traitors at home and especially the Jews. If only they can get a strong leader they will win next time…

1930s

1933 German elections won by the National Socialist party – Nat-so, or-Nazi party, for short. They are led by mad, bad Adolf Hitler. They begin bullying Jews and building up stocks of weapons. The Germans have enemies – especially Mr Stalin's Soviets – but they have friends like Mr Mussolini's Italy. Mr Churchill of Britain tries to warn the Brits but no one takes much notice … yet.

1937 In Europe two rival 'teams' are forming – the 'Allies' of Britain, France and the Soviets against the 'Axis' of Germany and Italy. The teams are spoiling for a match.

Over in Asia the Japanese attack China. So what? So their war will get mixed up with the war in Europe that is coming soon...

30 September 1938 Britain and France agree with Germany and Italy there'll be no more war. 'Peace in our time!' says Brit Prime Minister Neville Chamberlain. Fat chance.

5 October 1938 Adolf Hitler's Germans take over the Sudetenland in Czechoslovakia ... peacefully. 'I am just protecting the three million Germans who live there!' he says innocently. (Rearrange the letters of 'A. Hitler' and you get 'The Liar'!)

23 August 1939 Shock! Deadly enemies unite! Mr Adolf Hitler of Germany (with a toothbrush moustache) and Mr Josef Stalin of the Soviet Union (with a yard-brush moustache) peacefully agree not to fight one another. No chance. Never trust a man with a moustache.

1 September 1939 A. Hitler (the liar) had promised not to invade Poland. Today his army invades Poland ... and 'peacefully' shares it with the Soviets. No one asked the Poles, of course. Britain and France say they'll fight for Poland's free-dom. That means war!

148

3 September 1939 Britain and France declare war on Germany. Next day Mr Winston Churchill (who doesn't have a moustache or much hair at all) is made First Lord of the Admiralty. He could say, 'I told you so!'

8 November 1939 Six people killed when a bomb explodes in a Munich beer hall. It was meant to kill Hitler – but he left fifteen minutes before it exploded. Hitler lives – millions will now die in the Second World War.

1940

9 April Germany invades Denmark. The Danes are so surprised they don't fight back.

10 May Brits make Winston Churchill their Prime Minister. 'I have nothing to offer but blood, toil, tears and sweat,' he says. And the

149

blood and tears of millions of others too, of course. On the same day it's the blood and tears of the Belgians and Dutch as Germany invades.

June Brit armies in France driven back to the beaches at Dunkirk. They escape. Mr Churchill says Brits will defend themselves in the streets and the hills if the Germans invade. 'We will never surrender!' Tough talk for tough times. Italians (who think they know a winner when they see one) join Germany in war against the Allies.

14 June Germans enter Paris. The French say, 'We gave up without too much of a fight because we didn't want our lovely city destroyed.' Germans sneer at this feeble excuse.

7 September German planes bomb London in daylight while British Royal Air Force hit dozens of

150

German cities. Women and children are now in the front line of war.

December Now Japan joins in the war on Germany's side. Italy invades-Greece – just like the ancient Romans all over again – and Egypt. This is the start of war in the deserts of North Africa.

1941

10 May Mad Hitler's madder assistant, Rudolf Hess, pinches a plane and flies to Scotland. He wants to persuade Churchill to share the world with Hitler. The Germans say Hess is potty – and many Brits agree. The Brits lock Hess up for the rest of his long life. The next day German bombs destroy Brit House of Commons.

22 June Hitler breaks his promise to Stalin (surprise, surprise), and invades Russia. Hitler makes some

151

big mistakes but this is probably the biggest. The Soviets aren't going to give up as easily as some.

7 December Japanese warplanes bomb the US navy in Pearl Harbour, Hawaii. US goes to war with Japan in the Pacific Ocean. Then the Japanese capture the Brit colony, Malaya. Now there's a jungle war.

11 December Germany and Italy declare war on the USA. This is really becoming something you can call a World War.

1942

20 January Nastiest of all Nazi plans. German leaders meet and agree that Jews are not really human. Fit Jews will be worked to death and weak Jews will be starved or killed in death camps.

30-31 May RAF does more damage in one night raid on Cologne than 1,300 previous attacks (it says). Meanwhile, the Soviets have pushed back the German army and the US bombed the Japanese navy. The war is turning against the Nazis.

7 August In the Pacific, US marines land at Guadalcanal in the Solomon Islands. Now the war is turning against the Japanese.

4 November In the North African desert the British drive back the German tanks at the battle of El Alamein. That cheers up the Allies.

2 December A nuclear reaction is created by scientists on a Chicago squash court. If this power can be turned into a bomb it could win the war. From squash court to squashed enemies. But who'll build that nuclear bomb first? The race is on.

1943

February Germans finally defeated at Stalingrad, Russia. The Soviets start the long and bloody push towards Berlin.

19 April Jews in Poland rise up against the Nazi exterminators. A year ago they helped the Nazis to 'evacuate' fellow Jews to the camps because they thought it was for the Jews' own good. Now word gets back that they are, in fact, death camps. The rebels have little to lose – die fighting or die in gas chambers. But…

16 May Jews in Warsaw wiped out. Some prefer to die in their burning buildings or jump from the roofs rather than become Nazi prisoners. Hitler's assistant, Himmler, orders the destruction of Jewish settlements everywhere.

17 May RAF destroy German dams

with clever invention, a bomb that bounces on water. They wreck power supplies to German factories – and drown a lot of innocent people. Do not try this in your bath – either the bombing OR the drowning!

23 July Allies are back in Europe for the first time since Dunkirk in June 1940. They capture Palermo in Sicily and head north. It's a long way – and nearly two years – from Berlin.

25 July Italy's Benito Mussolini is thrown out of power as Italy is invaded by the Allies. Well, they have to blame someone.

1944

April In the Pacific the US are 'island hopping' towards Japan. In Europe the Soviets have reached Poland and Romania in the fightback to the north and east of Germany. Their Brit and US allies are heading north through Italy. All they need is an attack through France to the west and, guess what…

6 June D-Day. Allies land in France and head towards Berlin. But they're still almost a year away.

12 June New German secret weapon, a flying bomb, lands on London. It's called the V1 – 'V' for Vergeltungswaffen … vengeance weapon. Within a month almost 3,000 Brits will be killed by them. Some weapon, some vengeance.

20 July Now Hitler himself is bombed – by his own German Army officers. The bomb blows Hitler's trousers off but sadly he survives.

31 August The gallant Poles rebel to throw out German invaders … again. But their Soviet and American 'friends' refuse to help them. Result? Poles poleaxed.

September First US troops set foot on German soil but the Germans fight back furiously. The end is still a long way off.

1945

27 January Soviets march in to Auschwitz concentration camp and free 5,000 prisoners, mainly Jews. But they're three weeks too late to save the last four prisoners executed for hiding explosives. All four were young girls.

14 February After two days of Allied air raids the ancient German city of Dresden is flattened. Statues, paintings and beautiful churches are destroyed … and a small matter of 130,000 people. Happy Valentine's Day, Dresden.

12 March A 14-year-old Jewish girl finished her diary three months ago with the words, 'All people are good.' Today she dies, half starved and in a fever in Belsen concentration camp. But her diary lives on as a terrible warning to us. Thank you, Anne Frank.

28 April Italy's dictator Mussolini is tried. 'Let me live and I'll give you my empire!' he begs. Fat chance. He's shot and hanged by the heels for the people to see.

30 April Allies surround Berlin. Adolf Hitler doesn't want to end up like Mussolini. So he kills his dog, then his new wife Eva and finally himself. Guards burn the body to stop it being paraded by the conquering Soviets. Many Germans refuse to believe he's dead – many more believe it and kill themselves.

HE WAS ALWAYS BARKING

I'VE GOT A BAD FEELING ABOUT THIS

7 May New German government surrenders and the war in Europe is over. But the most fearsome drama of the war is still to be acted out.

6 August US drop first nuclear bomb on the Japanese city of Hiroshima. When a second bomb destroys Nagasaki three days later the Japanese surrender. It's hard to fight an enemy when a single bomb can kill 60,000 people in seconds. The Second World War ends five years (and 40 million corpses) after it started.

ZIP

Home horrors

The Second World War was different to past wars because you weren't safe anywhere. Innocent young people could be lying in bed reading a comic or studying at school or sitting on the toilet one moment – and be dead the next.

Bombs could blast you, saboteurs could spifflicate you and missiles marmalize you wherever you were. A battle area was known as a 'Front'. Now countries outside the war zones had their own 'Home Fronts'.

Horrible history happened at home as well as on battle fields...

Dad's barmy army

In Britain in 1940 the people were worried about a German invasion from the sea and from the air. The brave Brits started to arm themselves with shotguns and any weapons they could lay their hands on.

The government decided it would be better to organize these fighting folk into a proper army. In 1939 Winston Churchill had wanted a Home Guard formed – when he became Prime Minister in May 1940 he got it. Churchill had hoped for 500,000. He got 250,000 in the first day and 1,500,000 by June. They were first known as the Local Defence Volunteers – the LDV.

At first these untrained men were a bit of a joke. They weren't given proper weapons, they just armed themselves with anything that could kill. One boy said:

We were sent to defend a factory with broom handles. I pinched a knife from Mum's kitchen and tied it to the top.

One 14-year-old boy took along a bow and arrow. That would have worried some German tank commander if the Germans really had invaded! Others took along a nice heavy golf club.

No wonder a popular comedian, George Formby, sang a song about them...

I'm guarding the home of the Home Guard,
I'm guarding the Home Guard's home.
All night long, steady and strong,
Doing what I told 'em, I can't go wrong.
One evening when on LDV,
Some German soldiers I did see.
They ran like Hell ... but they couldn't catch me!
I'm guarding the Home Guard's home.

PLINK
PLINKA
PLINK

The government said Home Guard soldiers had to be aged between 17 and 65. But boys as young as 14 joined. Some old soldiers from the First World War lied about their age and were eighty years old. No wonder they got the nickname 'Dad's Army'.

The men in Dad's Army were keen. It was great that they felt they were doing something to help. But sometimes they were too keen and too clumsy. Then they became Dad's disasters…

Ten horrible Home Guard facts
1 Home Guard soldiers were worried about how to spot a German. They were warned an enemy paratrooper might be disguised as a nun, a vicar or even a woman carrying a baby. The daftest idea for uncovering a spy was to shout…

…and a German couldn't stop himself from raising his arm, clicking his heels and replying…

2 Home Guards were in more danger from their own weapons than from the enemy who never arrived. They were given sticky bombs – a bit like explosive toffee apples on a stick. The idea was that they would run up to an enemy tank and slap the goo-covered bomb on to the side. But many tried to *throw* the bombs, the sticks came loose and the bombs fell at their feet. Oooops! 768 Home Guard members were accidentally killed during the Second World War and nearly six thousand more were injured.

3 And their families were also at risk. A Home Guard soldier was cleaning his rifle on the kitchen table and forgot that there was a bullet in the firing chamber. He pulled the trigger, the gun went off – and killed his wife.

4 Early in the war Home Guard soldiers seemed to believe that anyone landing by parachute must be a German. A brave RAF pilot, James Nicholson, was hit by canon fire from a German fighter. His foot was smashed and he was on fire. He stuck to his task and shot down the enemy plane before parachuting clear. As he drifted down, wounded and burning, some young Home Guards began blasting at him with shotguns. He screamed at them to stop but they were too excited to listen. Somehow he survived but was more injured by his Home Guard colleagues than by the enemy attack. (James Nicholson became the only Second World War fighter pilot to get the top medal, the Victoria Cross, for his action that day. His Home Guard attackers didn't get medals.)

5 Home Guards had to deal with reports of spies, even when those reports were a little wild. A British officer was sent to live in Winchester and was given a room in a nearby village with a vicar. The vicar's daughter immediately suspected him of being a German spy and ran to report him to the Home Guard…

You can tell that girl was keen to flush out spies!

And an old woman locked a man from the electricity board in her cupboard because he had a little moustache like Hitler.

6 School children weren't safe … not even from their school mates. Alan Chadwick enjoyed going down to the local aircraft factory after school to watch the new planes being tested. A 17-year-old Home Guard was on patrol to stop spies. As Alan cycled by the fence the guard called him to stop. Alan ignored him. The guard called again and when Alan took no notice he fired a warning shot into the ground. But the bullet bounced off the road, hit Alan in the back and killed him. Why hadn't Alan stopped when the guard called to him? Because he was deaf.

163

7 Some Home Guard soldiers saw themselves as a wartime police force. They set up road blocks to stop and question everyone who came that way. One man complained he was stopped twenty times on an eight-mile journey!

Even a local milkman was sent home to get his identity papers. A Scottish man on the Air Raid Protection team was driving to Leuchars air base one night when he ignored a Home Guard road block. He was shot dead.

8 A government inspector was measuring a field one day when local villagers accused him of being a German spy. An old farm worker tried to protect the inspector and was shot and killed by a panicking Home Guard member. The harmless old man was 68 years old. The inspector tried to show his identity papers but he was killed too. The soldier who shot them went to prison for twelve months. During the Second World War 50 innocent Brits died at the hands of their own Home Guard.

9 Of course it was probably worse being a member of the Home Guard in Germany. A 59-year-old farmer, Karl Weiglein, was called to serve in the Nazi home defence army towards the end of the war. As the enemy drew near the Nazis blew up a local bridge and that annoyed the farmer. He complained to one of his neighbours, 'The people who did this are idiots and ought to be hanged.' But the Home Guard commander (the local school teacher) overheard old

Karl. He arranged to have him tried and then executed. The old man was hanged from his own pear tree outside his own front door while his wife watched from the window. The body was left hanging for three days as an example to anyone else who wanted to complain.

10 The French Home Guard (The Franc-Garde or the *milice*) was set up to check on illegal food supplies. If a restaurant had more food than its ration the *milice* shared it around the poor. Sounds friendly? In fact the *milice* made themselves into an extra police force, working for the German army who were occupying France. They raided homes, spied on neighbours and betrayed freedom fighters to the enemy forces. A French survivor explained…

> *When you walk through French streets there are blue signs that say, 'Jacques Dupont was shot here by the Germans.' But they never say, 'Jacques was first betrayed by Frenchmen working for the Nazis.'*

The British 'Dad's Army' could be a danger to themselves and to the British people … but other Home Guard armies could be far more cruel.

Secret army
By 1942 the British Home Guard were given proper training and good weapons. No one knows how much use they'd have been if Britain had been invaded. But there was another group of fighters who would have had a good chance against invaders.

They were a secret army of highly trained commandos who were given the very best weapons and underground hide-outs. How did this special force stay secret? Was it because…

a) They only trained at night when everyone was asleep?

b) They trained on a deserted island off the coast of Scotland where there were only sheep to spy on them?

c) They pretended they were ordinary Home Guard soldiers?

Fighting French

In 1940 the Germans came to France and liked it so much they stayed. There were reports of German Officers shaving with champagne.[1] The Germans stayed in the north and east of France and ran it as if it were Germany – it was known as 'Occupied' France.

1. Actually they shaved with razors and just rinsed them in champagne, but you know what I mean.

They very kindly let the French run the south and west of the country from the town of Vichy – and that was known as 'Vichy' France. Of course, the French in Vichy France had to be well-behaved and act like little Germans or they'd be punished.

The Germans didn't want people from Occupied France going backwards and forwards to Vichy France, taking out secret information and bringing in weapons. The border was closed.

Oh, and there was a third bunch of French – the 'Free' French, led by General Charles de Gaulle who had escaped to England when the Germans arrived.

The German secret police (the Gestapo) made it pretty miserable in Occupied France, so secret groups began to resist German rule – they were the 'Resistance.'

Winston Churchill and the Brits decided to help the Resistance by setting up the SOE – (Special Operations Executive) – a group so secret that no one outside even knew it existed.

By 1942 they were secret agents in France to help make life tough for the Germans. While Soviet women fought in tank battles and the trenches, Western women didn't fight in the big battles of the Second World War. But they did play a brave and vital part in the Resistance.

Terrible traitors
In 1939, just before the war, there were three friends living in Paris: an Englishman, a Frenchman and a German.

There was the Nazi German, aged 50. He pretended to be a policeman on holiday, but was really there to find people who would spy for Germany when the war began.

There was the Englishman, aged 30. He had been to public school and become a newspaper reporter, but he really wanted to be a spy. When he tried to join British Military

Intelligence section 6 (MI6) they turned him down.

Lastly there was the Frenchman, aged 28. He was a brilliant pilot, and had been a trick flier in a flying circus as well as an airline pilot.

The war started and they went to their home countries (but during the war they secretly met up again in Paris).

France was soon occupied by Germany, and the German returned to France – this time to catch spies.

The Englishman took a job in SOE sending spies into France – but he didn't tell anyone about his friend, the German spycatcher.

And the Frenchman came to England and offered to work for SOE, flying spies in and out of France. He did admit he had a German spycatcher friend, but he said that would be a great help in dodging the Germans.

What would YOU do with the Frenchman? Give him a job? Or lock him away? The SOE gave him a job ... but of course his English friend was high up in SOE.

What happened? SOE flew in spies and equipment for a year. Then suddenly the Germans swooped and arrested all of SOE's agents – 1,500 of them. They had been betrayed.

Most of those brave 1,500 agents died after they'd been

tortured. But who betrayed them? Could it have been the Frenchman? He was put on trial after the war to explain himself and he might have been found guilty but someone spoke up for him – the Englishman!

The Frenchman was set free, the Englishman got an OBE award ... and the brave resistance fighters got a firing squad.

Terror for traitors

Germany occupied several countries and in every one they found some local people willing to help them – 'collaborators'. But not all collaborators got off as lightly as the traitors in the last example.

In Poland, a Resistance fighter described how he dealt with a collaborator...

A man who informed on us to the Germans lived in the village of Srednie Lany. We marked him down for execution. We went to his house at night, tied him up and made him give us the names of other Nazi informers in the surrounding villages. We also asked for the names of the people he'd betrayed. After that we called all the villagers together, read out the death sentence and carried it out on the spot. To protect the villagers against Nazi revenge I left behind a note which read: 'This is what will happen to anyone who works for the Germans.'

The Germans weren't popular in Poland. They took all the best food for themselves and the people of the occupied country went hungry. That's why they rebelled.

A Polish tax collector had the job of stapling metal tags to the ears of pigs to show they belonged to the Germans. Resistance workers entertained some villagers by grabbing the tax collector and fastening the tags through his ears. Ouch!

Women also suffered revenge attacks. A French woman fell in love with a German soldier. When the war was over the villagers came to get her…

When they came for me I thought they would break down the door. I was frog-marched into the street where men and women held me down. Their faces were twisted with hate and they called me a traitor. Then somebody grabbed a handful of hair and started hacking away with a pair of scissors. I tried to hide my fear but I almost choked when I saw the flash of a razor. It was scraped across my head painfully. The crowd were cheering and howling. They painted swastikas on my head using mud from the gutter. I have never felt so wretched in my life.

Of course it wasn't only in France that traitors were punished by their own people. In Russia a Resistance fighter wrote…

We shot a traitor. In the evening I went to do the same to his wife. We are sorry that she leaves three children behind. But war is war!

And murder is murder.

Fighting females

The heroes and heroines of the Resistance deserve a book of their own. These are just four examples of the work some heroines did and the things they suffered.

Name: Yvonne Cormeau

Code name: Annette

History: When her husband was killed in the London Blitz she joined SOE as a radio operator and parachuted into France. She was almost caught when agent 'Rodolph' betrayed her group. She received a bullet wound in the leg while fighting with the Resistance. She travelled through France disguised as a district nurse. When stopped at a German checkpoint her radio equipment was examined. She told the German guards it was her X-ray machine— and they believed her!

End: Survived the war. Died in January 1998, aged 88. Her blood-stained briefcase and dress with a bullet hole can be seen in the Imperial War Museum, London.

Name: Dianne Rowden

Code name: Paulette

History: An English girl who had lived with her parents in the south of France and loved the country. When the Nazis invaded she decided to try and help the French gain their freedom. She was landed in France in 1943 but didn't know that traitors had already betrayed her Resistance group. She was followed from the moment she landed, so every time she visited a contact she was accidentally betraying them! After a month the Gestapo arrested her and tortured her. She refused to talk.

End: In May 1944 the Allies were ready to invade Europe. The Nazis worried that Dianne could be freed and would tell the British who the traitors were. So she was taken to a prison camp in Germany. A doctor told her he was giving her an injection to protect her against typhus. In fact, he was injecting her with poison. Her body was 'evidence' so it was destroyed in an oven.

Name: Violette Szabo

Code name: Louise

History: Violette's husband was killed fighting with the Free French forces in North Africa. She decided to join the Resistance to avenge him. But Violette didn't want to be a radio operator – she said she wanted to 'fight with a gun in my hand.' After running into a German patrol in June 1944 her group fled but Violette twisted a weak ankle, injured in parachute practice. She held off the Germans while her companions escaped and was finally captured.

End: Violette was sent to Ravensbruck Concentration camp. She believed that being British would protect her, but in February 1945 she was taken from her cell and shot in the back of the neck. A book and a film called **Carve Her Name With Pride** were written to tell her story.

Name: Odette Sansom

Code name: Celine

History: Travelled through Vichy France carrying messages and codes for her group leader, Peter Churchill. When they were caught she tried a daring lie, saying she was married to Peter and they were related to British Prime Minister Winston Churchill. She was tortured to betray her secrets. First her toe nails were torn out one by one but she refused to talk. Then she was locked in an empty underground cell with no light and only a board to sleep on. As a child she'd been blind, so the weeks of darkness didn't frighten her either.

End: When the Germans were defeated Odette's lie about Churchill paid off. As the Allies approached the concentration camps many secret agents were executed to silence them for ever. But not Odette. The commander of her camp decided to take her to the Allied forces personally and say, 'Here is a relation of your Winston Churchill. I saved her. Take care of me.' She survived and became famous for her courage with a book and a film (both called Odette) about her war deeds.

Resistance dangers

Living in another country means more than simply learning to speak the language. There are dozens of ways you can give yourself away...

Oooops! 1 A woman SOE agent was parachuted into France from England. She arrived safely in a large town. But when she came to cross the road she looked carefully to her right ... and was almost knocked down by a truck that was coming from her left. She simply forgot that the foolish French have the crazy habit of driving on the wrong side of the road!

The good news is the truck missed her. The bad news is that a Gestapo officer saw what she did, guessed her secret, and arrested her.

Oooops! 2 'Annette' was dropped into the Gascogne region of France. It was the custom of women there to wear jewellery in public. 'Annette' arrived with no jewellery so she stood out. She also had to learn that the locals didn't sip soup from the side of the spoon and women didn't walk with such long strides as hers.

The clumsiest mistake was to give her a cover story that said she was from Occupied France in the north and had moved to Vichy France in the south. To do that she'd have to cross the border and have her papers stamped. The stamp was missing from her false papers. Somehow 'Annette' survived the careless way she was prepared.

Oooops! 3 Secret agents were given large amounts of money to carry into France. The money was to buy weapons and other equipment and make sure the resistance groups could buy food.

Freedom fighters in the Balkans area of Europe knew that British agents would land with a money belt stuffed with cash. So some of the agents were murdered as soon as they landed. The fighters said, 'Thanks for the money, we don't need you!'

One British agent, Nigel Low, had a criminal record for stealing money from his company before the war. He was trained as an agent, given a large amount of cash and dropped in France. He simply ran off with it and was never seen again. A case of...

Polish pain

When the Nazis invaded Poland in 1939 their friends (for the moment) the Soviets marched in from the east and took areas of Poland that used to belong to them 20 years before.

The Soviets didn't want the Polish Army to fight back, so in April and May 1940 they...

- took all the Polish officers to the forest of Katyn where there was a large pit dug amongst the trees
- shot the Polish officers in the back of the head
- threw them into the pit and buried them ten layers deep.

The Soviets then tried to cover the graves with freshly planted trees and the tracks leading to the grave were grassed over. Still, three years later, the German army discovered the mass grave.

Who did the Soviets blame? They blamed the Nazis who'd passed that way when they invaded Russia!

IT WASN'T ME GUV, HONEST!

Stamping out trouble

The Soviets also imprisoned enemies inside Poland. Anyone who had connections around the world was an enemy. So all of the area's stamp collectors were rounded up and ... stamped out.

When they later invaded Latvia their records show they shot a woman because...

She was caught singing a Latvian folk song

...while some Germans shot any Russian peasants who

could read and write. 'Anyone who is clever enough to read and write,' they said, 'is clever enough to cause trouble.'

The Soviet prison officers in Latvia were utterly brutal. Every prisoner who came to them was tortured. But they weren't the carefully planned tortures that the Nazis used. The Soviet jailers...

- beat prisoners with railings broken from fences
- crushed their fingers in the doors of their cells
- put thin books over their heads and beat them with hammers (because they wanted to cause pain, not death from a fractured skull).

One poor prisoner had his private parts wrapped in paper that was then set alight.

Whole families of Poles, Latvians, Lithuanians and Estonians were sent to Soviet prison camps in Siberia. The conditions in the trains taking them were so bad that when they stopped at stations the dead would be thrown out on to the platform.

When they arrived in Siberia things were worse. In temperatures of minus 40 degrees they had to live in holes in the ground or huts made of straw and branches. The men, women and children who survived the cold were worked to death.

When their German 'friends' invaded Russia in the summer of 1941, the Soviet jailers wiped out their prisoners in Poland with unbelievable cruelty. Sticks of dynamite were thrown in to one cell full of women prisoners. Another cell floor was found scattered with the eyes, ears and tongues of the dead prisoners.

The Soviets were as savage as their new enemies, the Nazis.

Winners and losers

For the first year of the Second World War the people outside the battle zones were hardly affected by the war. But the longer it went on the more difficult, dangerous and deadly it became, whether you were in Munich, Manchester, Milan or Moscow.

There were winners, and there were losers, as there are in times of peace.

Winners at war...

1 Coca Cola Coke had a 'good' war. It was supplied at a nickel a bottle to US soldiers. Coca Cola controlled 95 per cent of the overseas soft drinks market. During the war, US soldiers drank ten *billion* bottles. In 1939, Coca Cola had only five overseas bottling plants. By 1945, they had 64. What made it so popular? Because the water was so disgusting. The army kept it clean by adding chlorine – so it tasted like your local swimming pool. Sometimes water was carried in old petrol tanks or oil drums just to add to the flavour. Their powdered coffee was dreadful, fruit juice was known as 'battery acid' and 'lemonade crystals' made a drink that tasted of disinfectant. Alcohol was banned in the US forces – one tank crew got their hands on an enemy supply of champagne and almost ran over a jeep   a jeep carrying their general.

2 Cigarette makers If you want to get on in the war then own a cinema. People who went to the cinema smoked heavily in the 1940s. One owner went around and collected the cigarette ends from the floor, took out the tobacco and turned them into new cigarettes. They were named 'RAF' – perhaps because they were 'Really Awful Fags'. The manufacturer was sent to prison for his illegal manufacture of these killer weeds but his cigarettes still kept turning up at the Front ... so someone was still 'winning' during the war.

3 Black marketeers When food was scarce it often replaced money. It was against the law to trade food without ration books. People who did were known as racketeers and when they were caught in Germany they could be shot.

Three Nazi Ministers were suspected of being racketeers in 1944. They were investigated but their case was handled by Berlin's Chief of Police ... one of their racketeer friends! So, were they arrested, tried and punished? Don't be daft! Of course they weren't!

A Berlin waiter ran a 'Black Market' business – he could get things for people when they were in really short supply on ration – petrol, perfume, food and drink. This man made so much money he was able to retire to a big house with an estate in the country. He was rich but had taken great risks. Even people caught hunting through bombed ruins to take valuables were dealt with savagely.

4 The German chemical industry At the start of the war a German chemical company known as I G Farben was the largest in the world. But its huge success was based on cheating. While everyone else in the world had to pay their workers, I G Farben used slave labour. The concentration camps were packed with rounded up prisoners and I G Farben was able to pay the Nazis five Reichmarks a day for each prisoner they used – the prisoner, of course, got nothing but hard work and was basically a slave. The people who ran the factories argued with the people who ran the concentration camps...

Of course the result was neither fed the prisoners properly and they died quickly.

When the exhausted prisoners dropped down dead they were replaced with new prisoners. The Nazis built a forced labour camp at Auschwitz to provide slave labour for I G Farben's artificial rubber plant. The prisoners were fed thin turnip soup and bread that was full of sawdust. On average, they only survived for three months.

But some prisoners' fate was even worse than slavery and starvation. Scientists and doctors were allowed to use prisoners for gruesome experiments with new drugs and chemicals and surgery. At Auschwitz, Doctor Josef Mengele was obsessed by twins, and once sewed two gypsy children together to try and create Siamese twins.

In 1942 two prisoners did escape from Auschwitz and reported the death camps to the Allies. 'Please flatten them with your bombers,' they begged. But the Allies decided it would risk too many of their pilots and crew. The deaths went on.

...and war's losers

1 Vienna postmen Families in Austria tried to cheer up their fighting men by sending them chocolate and soap. But the army couldn't always deliver these so they sent them through the post. Chocolate and soap were scarce and valuable so a group of 17 postmen began opening the parcels, stealing the contents and selling them. The law enforcers of Vienna were not amused. The postmen were taken to the main square in Vienna and shot in public so everyone could see what happened to such despicable thieves. That's life – Postman Pat one minute, postman splat the next.

2 A Berlin family One Berlin family were definitely war losers ... they lost their grandfather! Here's how it happened...

So let that be a lesson. Wrapping wrinklies in wrugs is wrong!

3 German radio fans It was against the law to listen to foreign radio broadcasts in wartime Germany. Anyone caught would be punished.

What a silly law! How would the police know what you listen to in your own living room?

Er … actually there were little spies in German homes. Young people in the Hitler Youth organization were told they must report their parents if they listened to enemy radio.

Many Hitler Youth members did just that. An Austrian ballet dancer went to prison for three years after his daughter split on him.

Would you betray your poor parents? On second thoughts … better not answer that!

It wasn't just children who betrayed family. One woman told the Gestapo to listen under her window while her husband criticized Hitler – the poor man got four years in jail. It's cheaper than a divorce.

But how's this for gratitude…

But it was a dangerous game, informing on others. A railway worker lied about a woman neighbour and he was proved to be lying. He was shot.

4 The people of Leningrad In the winter of 1941-42 the Germans surrounded the Soviet city of Leningrad. Hitler decided not to waste German soldiers by entering a mined and booby-trapped city. He would use the ancient tactic of 'siege'. So the Germans surrounded the city, bombed it every day, and waited for the Soviets inside to starve and freeze to death. Many did.

In January 1942 a Leningrad doctor visited a family. He described what he saw...

A horrible sight met my eyes. It was a dark room, covered with frost and puddles of water on the floor. Laid out on some chairs was the corpse of a 14 year-old boy. In a pram was the body of a tiny baby. On the bed lay the owner of the room, dead. At her side stood her eldest daughter, rubbing her with a towel to try and revive her. In one day she had lost her baby, her brother and her mother, all perished with the hunger and the cold.

It's horribly true, but not surprising, that some of the starving people of Leningrad removed the arms and legs of the corpses and ate them. Cannibalism was the only way that some survived.

Yet the savage winter hurt the German attackers too. In time they were driven back and defeated. The starving of Leningrad may have been winners after all.

Firestorm fury

In a war you have to believe that you are fighting for the right side. When the Second World War started on 3 September 1939 the British Prime Minister, Neville Chamberlain, told his people:

> *It is evil things that we shall be fighting against – brute force, bad faith, injustice, oppression and persecution.*

In the USA in 1942 a poster showed the boxing champion Joe Louis with a rifle and neatly buttoned uniform saying:

"we'll win because we're on God's side"

The truth is that the other side believe exactly the same thing – and God doesn't usually take sides.

War is horrible but the Second World War was especially horrible because so many millions of *innocent* civilians were killed, bombed in their home towns, miles behind the battle front. Here are just ten gruesome facts about a bombing raid when the enemy destroyed a city without mercy.

Only one fact is wrong. Which one?

London – 13 February 1945

1 It was Shrove Tuesday and a carnival day. A day for children to forget the war, dress up in bright costumes and have a parade through the city streets. The circus was performing to a thousand happy families and there was no warning of what was to come.

2 First came the pathfinder planes. They found the city and dropped red marker bombs that hovered 200 metres above the city centre and marked the way for the bombers. Home Defence Fighters took off to shoot them down but the panicking gunners on the ground shot down their own planes. People who saw the flares ran for cover and the shelter of the cellars. But no air raid siren sounded.

3 The last act of the circus began and clowns rode donkeys into the ring. That's when the warnings finally rang out.

The first waves of a large enemy bomber formation have changed course and are now approaching the city boundaries. There is going to be an attack. The population is instructed to proceed at once to the basements and cellars. The police have instructions to arrest all those who remain in the open.

4 At 10:13 p.m. the first bombs fell. They were shattering high explosives that brought down buildings and trapped citizens in their shelters below the ground. But the worst was still to come. The fires, greedy for oxygen, sucked in air and winds rushed to feed them. The fires grew hotter, sucked harder, and the winds grew stronger and stronger

188

and stronger. This was the fire storm effect the bombers wanted. It was a whirlwind of flames that uprooted trees and sucked people off their feet into the heart of the fire.

5 The next wave of bombers arrived at 1:30 a.m. They were carrying fire bombs that spread a blazing liquid over the city and turned it into a massive bonfire. They had no trouble finding the city. They could see the fires from the first wave from two hundred miles away. This time the home fighter planes stayed on the ground. No one knows why – some think the links to their aerodrome were cut. The bombers had the freedom of the skies to drop their deadly fire bombs wherever they wanted. Of the 1400 enemy aircraft that flew over the city that night only six failed to return. As the circus tent collapsed in flames the dappled grey Arab horses huddled in a frightened circle. Their glittering costumes were seen shimmering in the light of the fires.

6 Wednesday dawned. Ash Wednesday. Survivors crawled out of the rubble that was once a city centre. A three-mile cloud of yellow-brown smoke drifted over the city and carried charred debris that fell on a prisoner-of-war camp 15 miles away. Ash Wednesday. Then the third flight of bombers arrived to rain down a further 11 minutes of death. Long range enemy fighters flew low and machine-gunned anything or anyone that moved. One plane machine-gunned a children's choir.

7 Some of the people in the cellars had weakened the walls that joined their house to the ones next door. When their escape to the street was blocked they broke down the walls into other houses again and again, looking for a way out. But smoke from the fires rolled down and choked them. An army officer, home on leave, saw sixty people in a cellar, their escape barred by a fire. He tried to help them…

SOAK YOUR COATS IN THE FIRE BUCKETS, PUT THEM OVER YOUR HEADS, AND RUN!

CERTAINLY NOT! IT'LL RUIN MY BEST FUR COAT!

The ones who refused to take his advice died.

8 One of the main targets had been the station. That morning children's bodies were stacked there in a huge mound. Many were still wearing their bright carnival costumes. But the station wasn't destroyed. By the next day the trains were running again. So tens of thousands of people had died and the enemy had gained very little.

9 Then the job of counting the cost began. For a week after the raid the city was filled with unburied dead. Bodies were lined up on the pavement to be identified. Rescue workers were given cigarettes and brandy to mask the smell. Prisoners of war were brought in to help with the work – but the citizens attacked them. They had to take their revenge on someone.

10 Bodies were buried in mass graves but there were no coffins and no sheets. Many were simply wrapped in newspapers, some in empty paper cement bags. There were too many dead to count. Some guesses say that it was 135,000.

Answer: Terrible but true. The only 'wrong' fact is the first word of the title. For this *wasn't* London destroyed by Nazi monsters. This was Dresden in Germany, bombed by the RAF by night and the US Air Force by day – with God on their side, of course.

190

Frightful fighting

Most of the fighters in the Second World War hadn't chosen to be soldiers ... they were normal people like your parents and teachers. (Well some teachers are fairly normal.) They joined the fighting forces and could be ordered to do some things they'd never have dreamed of doing in everyday life. Not just killing strangers – but killing them in some pretty nasty ways...

Shooting strangers

Sometimes you may be ordered to do something horrific in times of war. The trouble is you may have to spend the rest of your life with the terrible act on your conscience. Here is a true case. Imagine it happened to you.

- You are a British soldier in Burma, marching through the jungle towards the Japanese enemy.
- Your patrol captures three Burmese villagers and a ten-year-old boy who are almost certainly spying for the Japanese.

- If you let them go they will report your position to the enemy and the lives of all of your comrades will be in danger.

- The officer decides the Burmese must be shot and he selects you to be one of the firing squad.

What do you do?
a) Refuse and ask if someone else can do the shooting.
b) Agree to shoot the men but plead to let the boy live.
c) Obey. Shoot the three men and the boy.

The choice
You have *no* choice in fact.

If you **a)** refuse, then the officer could have you shot, and the four spies will die anyway.

The soldier in the actual story tried **b)**, and begged the officer to let the boy live. The officer explained that if the boy escaped he would betray them all and everyone could die. The boy would have to be guarded 24 hours a day and that would be difficult.

The soldier was forced to obey **c)**, even though the nightmare of the shooting lived with him 50 years after the event. He explained:

The boy faced us without a blindfold. As he was the second to be executed it meant he'd already seen his friend shot. When it came to his turn he was in a dreadful state. From close range the rifle fire made a terrible mess. It's something I've never been able to forget.

That's war. It affects the survivors as well as the victims. Many soldiers left the war with terrible memories like this.

Quick quiz

Fighting isn't the clean and tidy adventure it looks in many war films. Fighting can be disgusting. How disgusting? Can you guess the answers to these questions?

1 The British army sailed to Italy but many were sea sick. Where did they throw up?
a) Over the side of the ship.
b) Into wet paper bags that burst.
c) They shared a big oil drum that steadily filled up.

2 On Guam Island in the Pacific there were some unusual 'winners' in the battle between the Japanese defenders and the US attackers. What were they?
a) Frogs.
b) Flies.
c) Sharks.

3 The British fought the Japanese at Kohima in India and sheltered in trenches. What did they use as shields?
a) Dead Japanese soldiers.
b) Dead horses.
c) Boxes of Bibles.

4 American paratroopers were safer than British because…
a) They had springs in the heels of their boots to make landings softer.
b) They had two parachutes.

c) They were fatter and the fat protected them from being hurt when they landed.

5 The Germans chose non-smokers to go on patrol against the Soviets in 1941. Why?

a) Because non-smokers have a better sense of smell and they could sniff out the enemy.

b) Because smokers gave away their position with lighted matches and clouds of smoke.

c) Because smoke got in the eyes of the smokers and stopped them shooting straight.

6 German soldiers needed good boots for the Russian winter. After killing 73 Soviet soldiers their commander ordered them to take their boots. But the boots were frozen to the feet of the Soviets. What did the commander order?

a) 'Leave them.'

b) 'Soak them in petrol, set fire to them and thaw them out.'

c) 'Saw the legs off.'

7 The Italian commander in North Africa died before he could take charge of his forces. How?

a) He fell off a camel and broke his neck.

b) His plane was shot down by his own army.

c) He was bitten on the behind by a scorpion that was sleeping on his chair.

8 Why did a Nazi torturer in Paris work dressed only in his underpants?

a) Because the water torture would spoil his clothes.

b) Because the red-hot pokers had set fire to his trousers.

c) Because the Gestapo dragged him out of bed to question a suspect and he hadn't time to get dressed.

Answers:

1c) The soldiers were kept below the decks so they couldn't throw up over the side of the ship the way your dad did on the ferry to France. During the day they had the hatches above them open, but at night the hatches were closed and the air was suffocating. That's when many men were sick. They shared a large oil drum. As the ship rolled over the waves, the vomit sloshed around in the drum. *Slop – slurp – slosh!* (Hope you're not reading this just after your delicious school dinner?) When Allied troops sailed across the English Channel to invade France the American soldiers were given seasickness pills – the Brit soldiers were given paper bags. One commando said:

> *The landings were a success because the men would rather face the German bullets than face going back in those boats to be seasick again.*

2b) There were too many rotting Japanese corpses for the defenders to bury. The flies had a feast. On Guam there were thousands of frogs who usually fed on the flies … but the frogs couldn't cope! The flies simply swarmed all over the island. The US troops landed and used a strong fly repellent. It certainly kept the flies away, but the smell was so strong it led the Japanese straight to the American positions in the darkness. You had a choice – be eaten by flies or shot by the enemy.

3a) An officer wrote:

> *The place stank. The ground everywhere was ploughed up with the shell fire and human remains lay rotting as the battle raged over them. Men vomited as they dug in. In some of the trenches, rotting bodies of Japanese were used to form the parapet shield. It was almost impossible to dig anywhere without uncovering a grave or a toilet.*

4b) American soldiers jumped from their planes knowing that if their main parachute failed to open they had a spare. The Brits knew that if their parachute failed to open they would be scraped off the ground like strawberry jam. A popular paratroopers song made a joke of a parachute failure. To the tune of 'John Brown's Body' they sang:

> *He hit the ground, the sound was 'splat',*
> *the blood went spurting high,*
> *His pals were heard to say, 'Oh what a pretty way to die.'*
> *They rolled him in his parachute and poured him from his boot,*
> *And he ain't going to jump no more!*

The British Army said a second parachute would take up too much room. The truth was a second silk parachute would cost another £20 and the Army couldn't afford it. So the price of a British paratrooper's safety was less than £20.

5a) The Soviet peasant soldiers were good at hiding on the snow-covered plains – but they smelled awful. A sharp-nosed German could smell a bunch of Soviet soldiers before he saw them and had a better chance of killing them. The Soviets smelled of cheap tobacco and sweat. They also smelled of perfume that they used to kill lice in their tunics. That putrid perfume killed the lice but – if a German smelled it – it could also kill the Soviet soldier. By the way, Hitler hated tobacco and his Nazi scientists proved smoking causes cancer over 20 years before anyone else thought about it. If this Nazi science had been shared with the world then they could have saved millions of lives – which would have made a real change!

6c) Italian soldiers fighting alongside the Germans in the Russian winter had cardboard boots. The German boots weren't much better and they took Soviet army boots whenever they could get them. When they found boots frozen to dead Soviet legs their officer ordered them to saw the legs off below the knees. They carried the legs back to camp, put them in ovens for ten minutes and were able to remove the boots.

7b) Marshal Balbo flew from Italy to Libya but Italian anti-aircraft guns accidentally shot his plane down and killed him. The Italians didn't have a very happy time in the North African desert war. In September 1940 they set off in their tanks to attack the British. Unfortunately they lost their way, and drove round in a huge circle until they ran out of water and petrol. When they finally came face-to-face with the British army many Italian soldiers panicked and ran away. They were driven back into battle by their leader, General 'Electric Beard' Bergonzoli (honest, that's what they called him!). By early December they had been defeated. The Brits were surprised to find that the Italians were ready to be taken prisoner and many of them had their suitcases neatly packed and waiting to be marched off to prison. Electric Beard was shocked.

I TELL YOU WHAT JOCK, THERE'S SOME VERY STRANGE FACIAL HAIR IN THIS WAR

8a) The French Resistance radio operator, Didi Nearne, was arrested in 1944 and taken to be questioned by the Nazis. When she refused to give them the information they wanted she was sent to be tortured. The torture involved putting her in a bath of cold water and holding her head under till she began to drown. Then she was dragged upright and questioned. The torturer was stripped so he didn't get wet – but he kept his underpants on because he was embarrassed by what Didi would see if he took them off. Despite the torture she didn't betray her group. Her nasty Nazi torturer asked, 'Did you enjoy your bath?' She had the courage to smile and reply cheekily, 'Excellent!' She survived.

Funny food

One way to win a war is to starve the enemy to defeat. Cut off their food supplies. Of course, the enemy is trying to do the same to you and your people at the same time.

Britain had to bring a lot of her food from across the seas so the German submarines set out to sink the food ships. The Brits suffered. The German people suffered even worse hardships than the British.

So, if you can't eat what you want, eat whatever you can get. The US Army gave its soldiers a book with this advice…

THE BLUEJACKETS' HANDBOOK Page 21

SURVIVAL

When you're far from base and your rations are low then you can stay alive by turning to Mother Nature.

Remember!

- All animals are good to eat.

- Be careful about eating poisonous snakes.

- Maggots make good food.

- Grasshoppers are tasty but pull the legs and wings off before eating them.

- Do not eat caterpillars.

Isn't history amazing? That last piece of advice is sixty years old but it's still useful today. Next time you're in a cabbage patch and feeling peckish remember *not to eat the caterpillars* – with a little digging you could find a few juicy worms.

US soldiers starving in Bataan found a rare food you don't get in burger bars. An officer said...

> *I came back from the front line and ran across three guys with a pot on the stove. I lifted the pot lid and saw a little bleached hand exactly like a baby's. It was a monkey.*

MONKEY SEE
MONKEY STEW

Would you have eaten a cute little monkey? You probably would if you'd been on the Bataan Hunger March. That was a forced march of 70,000 American and Filipino prisoners of war captured by the Japanese in the Philippines. Starting out on 9 April 1942, they were force-marched over 60 miles through the jungle. They were starved and often kicked or beaten on their way; many who fell were bayoneted. Only 54,000 reached the camp; 7,000-10,000 died on the way and the rest escaped to the jungle – where they ate monkeys or starved.

The Japanese officer who organized the march was executed after the war for his cruelty.

Hunger horror

The most famous diary from the Second World War was written by the Jewish girl who hid from the Nazis, Anne Frank. But she wasn't the only child to keep a record of her suffering.

A Dutch boy, Robert de Hoey, was living in Java with his family when the Japanese invaded in 1942. His father was sent to one prison camp while he and his mother were taken to another. For three years they suffered terrible hunger, yet survived. This is a translation from Robert's diary.

Day 1

Arrived at the camp and were told to wait for the camp's commandant. We were made to stand to attention on the football field for two hours in the baking sun. Babies cried, people fainted but no one was allowed to sit down.

Day 73

I think of food all the time. How can I stop? We play and we sleep, that helps. Day by day the rations have grown a little less. You hardly notice, then you remember how it was when we arrived. Our evening meal is usually thin vegetable soup and boiled rice. To get more food we try to grow it — carrots, onions cabbages, tomatoes. But we have to guard them because even the guards try to steal from from us.

Day 236

Mama has decided that I am old enough to help around the house. She's given me the job of keeping the toilet clean. With all the diarrhoea, and so many people using it, the thing is a disgrace. There is pee down the walls and even smears of poo. But I don't mind. I have my own mop and it feels like a real job.

Day 377

An important day. A food parcel has arrived from the Red Cross. This is good because we ate all the cats and dogs months ago. And it is no use hunting rats. Food is so scarce here even the rats have moved out. We shared a can of Spam between five people, I had ten raisins, three dried figs, a cigarette and a piece of chocolate the size of a postage stamp. I swapped my cigarette for another ten raisins.

Day 580

It is hard. Every day I see my fellow prisoners with bleeding gums holding broken teeth. Hair only grows in tufts, our stomachs are bloated from hunger and disease. Some have boils the size of table-tennis balls and others have raw ulcers weeping on their legs. No one has the material to spare to make bandages.

Day 701

They say the war is ending. Some brave women have smuggled radio parts into the camp. They'd be executed if they were ever caught. But the news is that Japan is facing defeat by the Americans. Every day we wait for the end. I can't remember what it was like being free and having enough to eat.

Day 727 (last day)

Word went around last night that we should meet on the field. But we are never allowed out after dark. We'd be shot.

I could see no guards. But in the moonlight
I could see the camp gates swinging open.
None of us left. We didn't know where to go.
Then, this morning, English officers marched
in. We began to bow to them the way our
Japanese guards had trained us. The English
made us stop.

Freedom Day 3

This afternoon my father came through
the camp gate. Mama said he was
coming. I hadn't seen him for three and
a half years. I didn't recognize him. He
hardly knew me or Mama. But we are
together.

The nightmare is over.

———

War game

It's all very well reading history books about the war, but you're safe and warm in your cosy classroom, with your friendly history teacher to help with the long words. You even sit on super-comfortable chairs. You have no *idea* what some people went through during the war.

Of course, you could get your local army camp to put you on a firing range and use you for target practice, but don't expect them to give you a gun to fire back.

So how do you get a real feel for the war? A US soldier at Guadalcanal in the Pacific fought in the trenches in torrential rain and suggested we should all try the following game:

Dig a hole in your back garden while it is raining. Sit in the hole while the water climbs up round your ankles. Pour cold mud down your shirt collar. Sit there for 48 hours and, so there is no danger of your dozing off, imagine that a guy is sneaking around waiting for a chance to club you on the head or set fire to your house. Get out of the hole, fill a suitcase full of rocks, pick it up, put a shotgun in your other hand and walk on the muddiest road you can find. Fall flat on your face every few minutes.

> *Snoop round until you find a bull. Try to sneak around him. When he sees you run like hell all the way back to your hole in the back garden. If you repeat this every three days for several months you may begin to understand.*

I-spy

Spies have been around for thousands of years but they become really useful in wartime. In the Third World War (due to start in the year 2033 when Martians invade) you may like to be prepared with one or two Second World War tricks.

Spycatchers were always looking for secret messages being passed to the enemy. The Germans had a hugely complex machine made to make unbreakable codes – but the Brits got a copy of the machine and cracked thousands of top secret messages.

You don't always need clever machines for complicated codes. Two people beat the spycatchers with simple ideas. Next time you need to send that secret message to a friend try one of these genuine Second World War systems...

Comma code

Flight Sergeant Graham Hall was a terrible writer. He never used punctuation in his writing. He once joked to his wife, Vera, 'If I am ever taken prisoner and I send a letter with punctuation, then you should underline the next word. It will be a coded message.'

In June 1940 his bomber was shot down and the crew were taken to one of the famous Stalag Luft Prisoner of War (POW) camps for airmen, in north-eastern Germany. Sergeant Hall wondered if his wife remembered their joke and he tried it. It worked so well that the British secret service used him to send and receive messages from the camp – news about German weapons and troop movements, requests for help with escapes and for equipment.

You can try it. Here's an example of how it might have worked…

Dear Vera

I am alive and well. Escape from plane was dangerous. Planned to celebrate my birthday, night after we crashed. 22nd birthday if you remember. September in the garden is lovely and I'll miss it. Send my love to sis, ma, pa, N.D Jones and my other friends at the pub, local. Money I owe them will have to wait.

Love

Graham

207

Someone as clever as you does not need to have the message worked out, do you?[1]

The prisoners of war were allowed to receive parcels and letters from home through the Red Cross organization. They also received games like Monopoly and chess to pass the time. What the Germans didn't know was the games were specially altered to send in secret supplies – silk maps in the monopoly board, radio valves in chess pieces and hacksaw blades hidden inside a pencil. A pack of cards was actually a map in 52 pieces.

Lemon aid

One of the great secrets of the war was the Nazi concentration camps. Even German people believed that Jews were just being sent to work for the Nazi war effort. The real horror was hidden from them. Letters from the camp were destroyed if they hinted at the dreadful conditions.

But some clever prisoners managed to smuggle out the truth using the old spy trick, invisible ink.

Try it yourself. Write a postcard with a simple message, then add the real message in invisible ink.

1. But for the dumb or the lazy reader, the message says, 'Escape planned night 22nd September send map and local money.' An escaper would need 'local money' once they were outside the camp and a map to find their way to the coast.

Lemon Spy!

YOU NEED THE JUICE OF A LEMON, A THIN PAINTBRUSH AND A PIECE OF PAPER

DIP YOUR PAINTBRUSH IN THE LEMON JUICE AND WRITE YOUR MESSAGE. PUT MORE LEMON JUICE ON THE PAINT BRUSH AFTER EVERY LETTER.

LEAVE THE MESSAGE TO DRY THEN SEND IT

WHEN YOUR FRIEND WANTS TO READ YOUR MESSAGE THEY JUST PUT IT FACE DOWN IN THE OVEN. (THE OVEN SHOULD BE HEATED TO 175°C OR GAS MARK 4). IT SHOULD TAKE ABOUT 10 MINUTES

THIS WORKS BECAUSE THE HEAT OF THE OVEN BURNS THE LEMON JUICE BUT NOT THE PAPER. BURNING CHANGES THE LEMON JUICE AND MAKES IT GO BROWN

Concentration camp prisoners would probably not have lemons so they would have to use sweat, saliva or pee as invisible ink. They aren't so healthy – stick to lemon juice.

The postcards with secret messages were meant to be read and destroyed, but some survived. One was put on display in 1997. The card was a simple message:

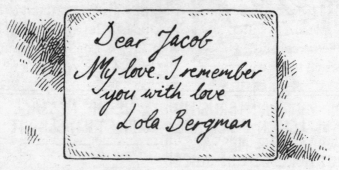

Dear Jacob
My love. I remember
you with love
Lola Bergman

But when the invisible message was read it gave a glimpse of the horrifying truth...

DEATH CAMP. THE REST
IS A LIE .HUNGER,
STARVATION, DOG FOOD,
OAT PORRIDGE. AN
EPIDEMIC. TORTURE.
TORTURE CHAMBER.
HUMILIATION. VIOLENCE
TERROR. FRIGHT
KILLING BY GAS.
EXECUTION. GALLOWS.
MURDER. INCINERATOR.
AGONIZING HELL.
OTTO.

It is believed that 'Otto' was Otto Haas, an Austrian who ended up in the death camp because he opposed Hitler.

Ruthless reprisals

Not all Germans were Nazis and not all Nazis were nasty. But there were times in the Second World War when the Nazis behaved as nastily as anyone in the history of the world.

One thing which seemed to bring out their viciousness was revenge. If one Nazi was hurt then a hundred innocent people had to suffer, to set an example to the rest. They were called 'reprisals'. On 22 March 1941 a London magazine carried this awful report…

The London Magazine

Nazi Atrocity in Poland

Following the death of a German soldier, one hundred Polish men were rounded up – most of them Jews – and marched through the streets with their hands tied behind their heads. They were ordered to dig their own graves and, to satisfy the barbaric cruelty of the soldiers, forced to perform a 'dance of Death' at the point of a bayonet for the Germans' amusement. There were various methods of execution, some shot, some hanged and others tied to posts and stoned to death.

Nazi violence wasn't only directed at the Jews. In Czechoslovakia in 1942 there was a similar act of cruelty…

Czechoslovakia Today

1 June 1942

Massacre at Lidice

Hitler's henchman, Reinhard Heydrich, was killed by a freedom fighter's bomb in the Czech capital Prague two weeks ago.

Heydrich – killed

Yesterday the German SS exacted their revenge on the small Czech town of Lidice.

They rounded up most of the 450 townspeople and shot 172 men. Seven women were shot as they were trying to escape and the rest were transported to a concentration camp at Ravensbruck. The 90 children were given new names and sent to Germany to be raised as Germans.

Today the SS will dynamite the town and the rubble will be levelled so that not a trace remains.

Of the women sent to the concentration camp, 52 died at Ravensbruck – seven of them exterminated by poison gas.

Two years later, in a French village, not even the women and children were spared…

FRENCH UNDERGROUND NEWS

Terror attack at Oradour-sur-Glane

Nazis may call their actions at the little village of Oradour 'revenge'– the rest of the world will call it bloody murder. The German forces massacred everyone they could find in the town and some 642 people were killed.

The Nazis marched into the town demanding to see identity papers and searched for explosives. The recent capture of an SS officer by the French Resistance fighters in the region had infuriated the Germans. Witnesses say the Germans herded the men into the barns and barred the women and children in the church.

Then the killings began. The 190 men were shot first and then smoke was seen rising from the farm houses as the SS bullies burned them. Finally the church was set on fire; women who tried to escape were machine gunned through the church windows and grenades thrown into the screaming masses killed many more. 207 women and children died.

Somehow ten lucky people survived by pretending to be dead till the SS left.

When the war was over a search was made for the Nazis responsible. In 1953 twenty were found guilty of a war crime at Oradour. Five were sent to prison – two were executed.

The abandoned village has been left in ruins as a memorial to the victims, with a single English word at the entrance of the village: Remember.

What made this tragedy even more horrible is that the Nazis had wiped out the *wrong* village. The German officer had been killed in Oradour-sur-Vayres, south of Limoges. The avengers killed the people of Oradour-sur-Glane, to the north of Limoges.

Test your teacher

It's amazing how much you don't know. And teachers, who look as though they lived through the Second World War probably know even less because their memories have begun to fade. (There are three things that happen to a person when they start to get old. First their memories go … and I've forgotten the other two.)

Anyway, torment a teacher or grill a granny with this quick quiz. All they have to do is answer 'true' or 'false'.

1 British and Allied troops coloured everything khaki brown as camouflage. They even had khaki toilet rolls!

2 Japanese soldiers collected the skulls of US soldiers, cleaned and polished them and sent them home as souvenirs.

3 Some spies in Germany were executed by guillotine.

4 British soldiers in Italy were given winter clothes and died of the heat.

5 In November 1940 a man called Lloyd was arrested in Britain for lighting a bonfire in his back garden.

214

6 Soldiers who had skived off school when they were kids were more likely to skive off from the army and run away from battles.

7 Old people's homes in Germany were closed because all the wrinkly residents had been called up to fight in the army.

8 Blind people in Germany were not allowed to marry.

9 If you were late for work in a German factory you lost all of that day's pay.

10 Italian leader Mussolini was said to look like Oliver Hardy of the Laurel and Hardy films.

Answers:

1 True. At first Brit soldiers had white knickers and hankies. But a quick flash of white could give them away to a sharp-eyed enemy. Everything was coloured muddy, khaki brown, even toilet paper … and pipe cleaners! United States Marines kept white vests, though, and they saved their lives at Guadalcanal in the South Pacific. The trapped men signalled to rescue planes by spelling out 'H-E-L-P' on the ground with their vests.

2 False. But what is gruesomely true is that US soldiers *did* collect dead Japanese soldiers' skulls. In September 1942 the US Commander of the Pacific Fleet ordered: 'No part of the enemy's body may be used as a souvenir.' The order was ignored. One US sailor sent a polished rib from a Japanese airman home to his sister. She'd begged him for it. Plundering gold teeth from their Japanese enemies was another charming hobby – and the victims weren't always dead. A burned Japanese head (still wearing its helmet) was paraded on a US tank at Guadalcanal – and you thought displaying enemy heads died out with the Celts fifteen hundred years before?

3 True. In August 1942 German spycatchers uncovered a team of 46 spies. They were sending radio messages to Soviet enemy agents. The Germans named the spy group the 'Red Orchestra' and soon put a stop to their playing. The male spies were taken away and hanged. But the females were executed using the French system of the guillotine.

4 False. The opposite was true. The army planners believed it would be very hot in Italy. But it was wet and cold. In the mountains it was freezing and many British soldiers in lightweight uniforms suffered terribly from the cold; some died. When the mud dried out, the roads and tracks turned to dust. Allied tanks raised great clouds of the stuff as they rolled forward ... and made clear targets for German guns. Cold or hot the Brits couldn't win!

5 True. Mr Lloyd liked the way Hitler did things and generally supported the Nazi party. He'd been thrown out of the army for his views. The bonfire was not a signal for enemy bombers but it was a gesture to show the Brits weren't going to tell him what to do. The magistrate gave Lloyd a prison sentence – Lloyd gave the magistrate a Nazi salute. If he'd had any sense he'd have said:

BUT IT WAS BONFIRE NIGHT!

6 True. At least it was true in the US army which did a survey. The Americans didn't like to call their men 'deserters', so those who ran away were said to be 'AWOLs' – short for 'Absent With-Out Leave'. Private Slovik was the only US soldier to be shot by his own army for deserting during the Second World War. The Germans, on the other hand, executed over 10,000 of their own men in the Second World War – and there were always plenty of volunteers to serve on the firing squads. (They executed 11 ordinary people in one day in 1942 for breaking the black-out rules!)

7 False. But this *was* a popular German joke! As the war went on and the fit men were killed or captured, the German Army called for older men and younger boys to join. 65-year-olds were called to serve in the German Home Guard and that gave rise to another German joke…

THEY SAY WE CAN GET OUT OF IT IF WE CAN PROVE OUR FATHERS ARE FIGHTING AT THE FRONT!

8 True. The Nazis were very harsh on people with handicaps. Deaf and blind people were not allowed to marry in case they produced deaf or blind children. And the mentally ill were exterminated. Hospitals found an extra 100,000 beds for wounded soldiers by 'helping' mentally ill patients to die. This began in September 1939 (under cover of war). The plan was given the codename 'T4'. The aim of this 'mercy killing' of mentally or physically handicapped adults or children was to ensure racial purity – Germany in the future would be free of sick people. The handicapped were secretly taken from homes and hospitals and murdered. Parents and families were simply told that their relative had 'suddenly died'. Rumours spread and in 1941, the Roman Catholic Archbishop of Munster exposed the Nazi murders in a sermon. Surprisingly, it was halted.

9 False. It was much, much worse. If you were late for work then you could be sentenced to three months in prison. (And you thought an hour's detention for being late to school was cruel!) By 1944 workers were having to work 60 hours a week (or 72 hours a week in aircraft factories). If you were asked to do overtime then you had a choice ... do it, or go to prison for 12 months.

I SUPPOSE A THREE WEEK HOLIDAY IS OUT OF THE QUESTION?

10 True. Mussolini was short and fat. When he started to go bald he had his head completely shaved. When he became ruler of Italy he wore a dark suit and a bowler hat. Somebody told him he looked just like Oliver Hardy – a comic idiot – so he began dressing in military uniforms instead. Mussolini rarely smiled or laughed – especially at Laurel and Hardy films.

Murderous mines

The Soviet Union joined the war on the side of the Allies in 1941 and its people fought as brutally as anyone in history. The Soviet Union lost an unbelievable number of its people – some Soviet historians say 43 to 47 million Soviet people died, if you include the effects of war like starvation and homelessness – that's as many people as there were in the whole of Britain at the time.

The Soviets weren't too fussy about how they fought or who died, so long as they won. The USA shot only one of their 19,000 deserters in the whole of the war, but the Soviets weren't so caring. Men who committed crimes, or ran away from the battle, were sent to punishment battalions and given suicidal jobs...

219

The good news is that a Soviet soldier who was wounded in one of these clearances would be forgiven. (Of course, he'd also be forgiven if he stepped on a mine and died. All hundred pieces of him would be forgiven.)

Angel of the minefield

The Brits in North Africa had a different way of getting across a minefield, it seems. In 1943 a soldier told this story...

North Africa
July 1943

Dear Elsie
        I know you worry about me,
out here in the desert, but I think I'm
going to be all right. It seems we have
some sort of guardian angel watching
over us. Yes, I know I've never been
religious, but after what I saw yesterday
I'm not so sure.
        We'd just laid a minefield in the desert
to stop the German tanks advancing. We
were supposed to lay tapes to show a
safe, zig-zag path through the mines
but the German shells began to fall

before we could do it. We had to retreat to our defences.

Behind the rampart we found a young, blond-haired officer, his helmet blown off and a shell splinter deep in his chest. He was propped up against a fence post, dead. Before we could bury him we heard an engine from out in the minefield.

When we looked over the top of our rampart we saw an amazing sight. A British truck was driving over the minefield towards us. It should have been blown to pieces but it started weaving slowly, left and right, and found the safe zig-zag path even though there were no markers!

When the truck driver finally reached us I asked him, 'How did you find your way across?'

'It was that young officer!' he said. 'The one with fair hair. He walked across in front of us.'

I stepped to one side and let him see

the corpse propped up against the fence post. 'Is that him?' I asked.

I thought the driver was going to faint, he went that pale. 'Yeah. That's him! What's he doing there?'

'He died quarter of an hour ago,' I said. 'It wasn't him that guided you to safety.'

'Then it must have been his ghost,' the driver moaned. He crashed the gears of his lorry and drove off. I've never seen him again.

We buried the officer, of course. But it's strange we all have this feeling he's out there somewhere watching over us. So don't worry, Elsie, I know that I'll get home safe. Love   Bill

Wild weapons

In wartime the side with the best weapons has an advantage. Potty profs and brainy boffins raced to create new ways of battering buildings, chewing up children, walloping women, splattering soldiers and pulverising pensioners.

The Brits invented Pykrete – a mixture of sawdust and water that was frozen to make a material tougher than concrete. Ships built of Pykrete would be unsinkable and win the war. The war ended before they could be built. Sounds daft – but it's terribly true.

Here are some of the Second World War's brightest brainwaves, all believed to be in existence. Some were just rotten rumours – while others were terribly true. Can you tell which are which?

1 The Molotov cocktail

2 The airblast gun

3 The swimming tank

4 The superfast rocket

THIS IS A BULLET-FIRING ROCKET THAT FLIES FASTER THAN A BULLET. IF IT FIRES BULLETS FORWARD THEN IT WILL CATCH UP WITH THEM AND DESTROY ITSELF

IT FIRES ITS BULLETS BACKWARDS TO STOP THIS HAPPENING

5 The submarine aircraft carrier

A SEA PLANE IS PLACED ON THE DECK OF A SUBMARINE AND SEALED IN A WATERTIGHT BOX

THE SUBMARINE SURFACES, THE PLANE IS UNWRAPPED AND IS FIRED FROM THE DECK BY CATAPULT

6 Exploding dogs

TRAIN A DOG TO LOOK FOR FOOD UNDERNEATH A TANK

STRAP A MINE TO THE DOG'S BACK AND SEND IT INTO A TANK BATTLE. IT WILL WALK UNDER AN ENEMY TANK AND DESTROY IT

Answers:

1 The Molotov cocktail. It may seem a stupid idea to attack a tank with a bottle of paraffin … but terribly true! Vyacheslav Mikhaylovich Molotov served in the Soviet war cabinet and they were desperate for weapons to stop the German tanks advancing. Molotov ordered the manufacture of millions of these simple bombs and they are still made by terrorists today – and still called Molotov cocktails.

Some of them worked. It isn't nearly as safe inside a tank as you'd imagine. In north-west Europe mud and ice were the enemies of UK tanks. In mud, it was known for tanks to churn themselves in until only the turret remained visible.

IF I'D WANTED TO BE IN SUBMARINES I'D HAVE JOINED THE NAVY

On ice, Churchill tanks and others which were not equipped with rubber-plated tracks (unlike the US Sherman tanks) became giant uncontrollable toboggans.

To be trapped in a tank on fire was fatal. The hatches were too small for a quick escape. A US officer described a tank fire…

A tank that is hit belches forth long searing tongues of orange flame from every hatch. As ammunition explodes in the interior, the hull is racked by violent convulsions and sparks erupt from the spout of the barrel like the fireballs of a Roman candle. Silver rivulets of molten aluminium pour from the engine like tears.

Germans called Brit soldiers Tommies and they nicknamed their tanks 'Tommy cookers'. US soldiers called them 'Ronson lighters' because of Ronson's advert that said their lighters 'light first time.'

So Molotov cocktails were simple, but deadly – if you could get close enough to a tank to throw it without being shot!

2 The airblast gun. A brilliant idea! Sadly it was just a rotten rumour spread around Germany. But it's such a good idea perhaps you could try it in your own classroom.

ADAM'S GOT AN AIR BLAST GUN DOWN THE BACK OF HIS TROUSERS

PTHRRRP

3 The swimming tank. Another daft idea – but terribly true! On D-Day, British 'DD Tanks' (Dual Drive) were launched from landing craft to 'swim' to the beach. Each tank had a canvas skirt and propeller. They were designed for a short journey over calm, shallow waters. 32 were set off. But the sea was rough and they were launched too far out because naval crews were too scared to go any closer to the beach. 27 sank like stones, drowning all the crews.

4 The superfast rocket. Another rotten rumour from the Germans – who seemed to believe it. You can see why. A really fast rocket could easily travel as fast as a speeding bullet. But ... if the rocket is travelling at (say) 1000 miles an hour then the bullets in its guns are also travelling at 1000 miles an hour before they are even fired. Fire those bullets at (say) 500 m.p.h. and they're then travelling at 1,500 m.p.h., aren't they? Er ... I think that's right. Never mind. The idea of a missile firing bullets is daft enough.

5 The submarine aircraft carrier. An absolutely crazy Japanese idea … but it was terribly true. And it worked! The Americans had bombed Tokyo so the Japanese made this plan to get revenge. On 9 September 1942 Japanese submarine I25 surfaced and the pilot, Nobuo Fujita, was sent off to drop fire bombs on the forests of Oregon. The idea was the fires would spread to the west coast US cities and create panic. Only one of his four bombs went off and the small fire was easily put out by the forest rangers. Nice try Nobuo, the only man to drop bombs on mainland USA.

6 Exploding dogs. A sick, sorry and stupid idea, but terribly true, and it worked … sort of. It was a Soviet idea. The dogs were trained and taken on to the battlefield where the Soviets faced the Germans. Each dog had a mine strapped to its back. They were released and ran straight under the tanks. Unfortunately … the dogs had been trained using Soviet tanks so, of course, they ran under the Soviet tanks. The tanks were blown apart and the dogs didn't look too healthy either.

Awesome animals

Animals don't start wars but they certainly suffer in them. Vegetarians and veterinarians may wish to skip this section.

Cruel for creatures?

1 In the First World War the British Army had won with the help of horses – they pulled the guns, carried supplies and made a tasty meal when food was hard to find. But by the Second World War horses had no chance. In September 1939, Polish Cavalry charged the German Panzer tanks. A German soldier said:

In a few minutes the cavalry lay in a smoking, screaming mass of dismembered and disembowelled men and horses.

2 Animals provided sport for bored soldiers. Horse racing was impossible but US soldiers who invaded Italy enjoyed gambling on beetle races instead.

- Each man had his own beetle and painted his 'racing colours' on the insect's back.
- A two metre circle was drawn on the ground.
- The beetles were placed under a glass jar in the centre of the circle.
- The jar was lifted.
- The first beetle to crawl out of the circle was the winner.

Top class racing beetles were bought and sold, a lot of money was won and lost gambling on the races.

3 As the war ended, and the Soviet army closed in on Berlin, the German defenders drew back to defend Tiergarten Park. In the park was a zoo. On the morning of 2 May 1945 soldiers began to surrender to the sound of starving and wounded animals. But a Russian remembered the saddest sound was an old zoo keeper – the last one left – weeping over the body of a huge hippopotamus. It had been killed by a Soviet shell.

4 When Dresden was bombed in 1945, 48 circus horses were killed and left by the river Elbe. The same raid had smashed the zoo cages. The vultures escaped and found the dead horses. Six weeks after the bombing people were still reporting seeing escaped monkeys and even a lion.

5 Adolf Hitler liked dogs. While he was fighting in the First World War he had a little pet dog called Fuschl and he trained it to run up and down ladders. (Somebody pinched the dog and he never saw it again – unless it was served up to him in a pie.) Then Hitler had Alsatian dogs as pets and his wartime pet was called Blondi. When Hitler's friends decided to kill themselves in 1945 old Hitler offered to test the cyanide poison to see if it worked. He fed it to Blondi. It worked quickly and fairly painlessly.

6 Hitler was a vegetarian and hated to see creatures suffer. Lobsters are best cooked by dropping them into boiling water, alive. Hitler hated to hear the screaming sound that they made when dropped into the water and passed a law saying they had to be killed with kinder methods. So it was a good war for lobsters as well as for foxes and deer because Hitler also banned hunting animals with dogs. Of course, it was fine for his Nazis to hunt down and murder humans!

TERRIBLY CRUEL! OUGHT TO BAN IT!

7 Hitler's chief mass murderer, Heinrich Himmler, was keen to have non-Germans put into concentration camps, tortured, experimented upon, gassed, shot, beaten or simply worked to death. Yet Himmler said…

> *Shooting birds and animals is not sport. It is pure murder. We Germans have always had a respect for animals.*

He even considered his SS killers[1] should wear bells at night so any little creatures would hear them coming, run away and

1. The SS (short for Schutzstaffel) were Hitler's personal bodyguard – by the end of the war there were 50,000 of them! Just how much body did the madman have to guard? They wore smart black uniforms and were taught to be ruthless and hard-hearted. This was the organization that executed people in concentration camps.

not be trodden on by accident. Himmler also said that he liked the medieval German custom of putting rats on trial and giving them a chance to behave themselves, rather than be exterminated. Some Nazi regions banned experiments on live animals – vivisection – while allowing experiments on live human victims in the concentration camps.

8 Soviet prisoners in Germany were always hungry. It was a real treat for them to catch a stray dog and eat it. The dogs were hard to catch … they didn't want to end up as dog meat. The starving Soviets begged their German guards to shoot the dogs for them. The guards didn't mind because they thought the dogs were pests and they made good target practice. When a dog was hit the hungry prisoners went crazy. A guard remembered…

When a dog fell the prisoners would fall on it and tear it apart with their bare hands, before it was quite dead. They'd stuff the heart, liver and lungs into their pockets to be eaten later. Then they'd light a fire and skewer pieces of dog meat on splinters of wood and roast it. There were always fights over the largest pieces.

231

Tails of the unexpected

The Second World War produced lots of strange animal tales too.

Miaow did she do that?

The miracle mouser of London's St Augustine's Church has amazed her owner, Rector Ross. Yesterday he climbed from the rubble of his church to tell of the white cat's purr-fect prediction.

'Faith has been with us for three years,' he told our reporter. 'She kept her kittens on the top floor of the church house. But three days ago she carried them all down to the basement and tucked them into a corner. Every time I carried them back up she took them down again. Then, last night we had a direct hit. The top floor was demolished. But I found Faith and the kittens safe in the basement corner.'

The People's Dispensary

For Sick Animals plans to give heroine Faith their silver medal. Even the Bishop of London admitted, 'It certainly makes us paws for thought!'

9 September 1940

Germans quackers for Freda

A Swiss visitor to London has told of a new secret weapon that the German townsfolk of Friedburg have to warn them of Brave Brit air raids. And it's not a marvellous machine – it's a feathered fowl.

The panicking poultry, a duck called Freda, rushed through the streets quacking loudly. The Friedburgers were so scared they took to their shelters – just in time! Because our brave boys in blue battered them with bombs a few moments later.

'The duck saved hundreds of lives!' the visiting Swiss watchmaker told our paper. 'The frightened Friedburgers are so grateful they plan to erect a statue to Freda.'

Of course, we Brits all know what Freda was quacking as she ran through the streets, don't we? 'The British are coming! Duck!'

30 March 1943

Dog-tired hero   12 November 1940

A British Army company in Egypt has its mascot back. The desert troops called the loveable mongrel dog Sandy (of course) but thought they'd seen the last of the mutt. The truck he travelled in after the battle at El Alamein was captured. The men were taken prisoner but the beastly Boche threw sad Sandy out to die in the heat of the desert days and the freezing nights.

Somehow the big-hearted hound walked 140 miles back to Alexandria. He even found his way through the maze of streets back to the company barracks. PTO

'It may look like a mangy mongrel but it's got the guts of a British Bulldog!' the Company Sergeant Major said proudly.

No one could accuse super Sandy of being bone idle!

Coo! What a bird!

Yesterday the best of British pigeons, Mary of Exeter, was awarded the Dickin Medal for outstanding courage.

Mary carried secret service messages from Europe back to Britain and on her first mission arrived back with a slashed breast following an attack by a German hawk. These feathered fiends are specially trained by the Boche to bash our brave birds.

Did Mary give up? Is Adolf Hitler sane? No! Two months later the daring dove was back in action and this time returned with pellets in her body and part of her wing blown off. But the vital message got through.

Back home in Exeter her pigeon loft was blasted by bombs but somehow marvellous Mary lived to fly another day.

Her handler, Robert Tregowan, said, 'The last time we found her in a field close to home, wounded all over her body and nearly dead with exhaustion. I think she'd have walked home if she'd had to.' She's one weary warrior who's really earned her corn!

27 February 1945

Mutt medal misery

When the Allied armies landed in Sicily (10 July 1943) an American dog called Chips really earned his dog food by attacking a concrete machine-gun installation. In spite of being wounded, Chips dragged an Italian machine gunner out by the arm and three others surrendered. Soldiers have sometimes captured these strongholds single-handedly, but Chips did it with no hands!

Later the same day he rounded up another ten Italians.

When news of the daring doggy deeds got back to the USA Chips was awarded a Distinguished Service Cross, a Silver Star medal and a Purple Heart medal – even though it was against army rules to give animals awards.

A commander argued:

Brave men shouldn't have to share their awards with a dog.

So Chips lost his medals. He'd probably have been happier with a bone anyway.

Lousy liars

The first victim in war is the truth. It is killed stone dead. People tell all sorts of lies if they think it will help them survive or win the war.

The Polish plot
German troops marched into Poland in September 1939 and that was the start of the Second World War.

But Adolf Hitler didn't want anyone to blame him and his Nazis for starting the war! So Hitler's Secret Service chief, Reinhard Heydrich, came up with a big lie…

THE POLISH ARMY STARTED IT! THEY ATTACKED US FIRST!

Heydrich's plan was given the secret code name 'Canned Goods' and this was how it worked…

TOP SECRET

Canned Goods

1. Take German prisoners and shoot them dead.
2. Dress the corpses in Polish army uniforms.
3. Scatter the bodies near the German radio station on the border with Poland.
4. Invite the world's newspaper reporters to the site.

> **SEE! WE HAD TO DEFEND OURSELVES. THEY ATTACKED US AND HERE ARE THE BODIES TO PROVE IT!**

It's hard to know if anyone was daft enough to believe this pathetic plot.

Rotten rumours

Want to know what really happened in the Second World War? Then *don't* ask someone who was there at the time! Everyone talked about the war – but there were so many lies that people began to believe them.

Tall tales

In war all sorts of superstitions are believed. Some Germans believed that whenever one of their houses was bombed then the wall where Hitler's portrait hung would remain standing!

> **SO WHY DIDN'T THEY STICK HIS PICTURE ON ALL THE WALLS AND CEILINGS?**

Here are some of the Allies' stories that went around during the Second World War. How many of these are true?

1 *British soldiers must pay for weapons and equipment they've lost in the defeat at Dunkirk*

2 *Japanese spies have planted broken glass in American bandages!*

3 All women volunteers for the US Women's Army must take off their clothes and be inspected by male officers

4 British soldiers fighting in North Africa know they are safe when relaxing with a game of football. Germans

5 The Germans are short of meat and eating so many vegetables they're turning green!

6 A dog in Hawaii is barking messages to a Japanese submarine in morse code.

7 The Ford Motor Company will give a new car to the first 100 US Marines to land in Japan.

8 The British army in the Sahara desert has ordered a million sandbags. But they arrived already filled with sand.

9 Every time the Germans launch a V1 flying bomb they have six men killed by the take-off blast.

10 Scottish soldiers will be going home after the war in ships with tartan funnels!

Many US soldiers believed they'd get a free Ford car when the war was over – what in fact they each got was a free paperback book. (Not quite the same thing.)

Who started these stories? Sometimes a government decided to upset the enemy by spreading the rumours. For example the 'British Political Warfare Executive' invented them and passed them to travellers or foreign newspapers. They also spread 'good news rumours' in Britain. This one was believed by a lot of Brits…

1. The truth is that experiments with blazing petrol did take place but luckily the idea was never needed.

Did you know…?

Even after the war strange rumours circulated. Many refused to believe Hitler killed himself in his Berlin bunker. There were hundreds of stories about him being alive and well. Some of the strangest said Hitler was…

- living as a hermit in an Italian cave
- living as a shepherd in Switzerland
- working in a gambling casino in France
- working as a fisherman in Ireland
- still at sea, having escaped on a U-boat
- living in an underground hideout in Sweden with enough tinned food for years
- running a laundry in Germany
- working as a waiter in a Dutch coffee bar.

The last reported sighting of Hitler was in 1992.[1]

True lies

The US Government also had a 'Department of Liars' (called the Morale Operations Section). They spread a story that a terrible catastrophe would happen in Japan in August 1945.

1. It's all nonsense— along with the reports that he became a London traffic warden. The truth is he escaped to become an English teacher in the north of England. I know. He taught me.

240

No one told the 'Department of Liars' about the secret atomic bombs. On 6 August the first atomic bomb landed on Hiroshima. A lousy lie had strangely become the terrible truth.

It helps the war effort if you can learn to really hate the enemy – make them seem like savages who have to be defeated at all costs. A common US story concerned a US soldier who wrote home from a Japanese POW camp...

... but I'm OK and well looked after. Don't worry.
Love to my kid brother. Why not soak off the stamp on this envelope for his collection?

All my love
Hank

When the mother soaked off the stamp there was another message written underneath it...

They have cut out my tongue!

Some prisoners of war were tortured but this particular story is horrible, but untrue. How do we know? Because POW letters didn't have stamps!

Germany had its own terrible tales that were told to children. Here's a version of a cheerful bedtime story you might like to tell to a little brother or sister ... if you really hate them that much!

Hamburg horror – a grim fairy tale

The little girl limped down the bomb-ruined road, past the hollow houses and stepped carefully round the rubble. She was as thin as the rain that fell and the soles of her shoes were thinner. She clutched a small loaf of black bread to her thin chest.

It was growing dark and she wanted to get home before night fell and the rats came out. Even if they'd been working the twisted lampposts would not be lit. She stopped. There was a soft, regular click coming from a side alley. She froze and turned her head slowly towards the noise.

A man in a heavy army coat carried a white stick and was groping his way towards her. She stepped back and a stone clattered at her feet. The man stopped, raised his white face and eyes covered by discs of dark glass. He said, 'Is someone there?'

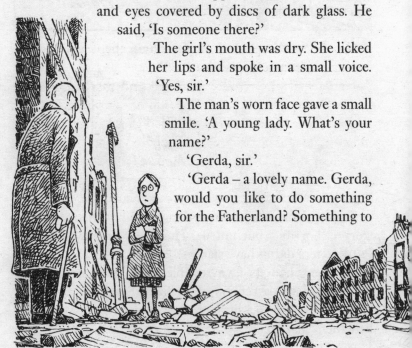

The girl's mouth was dry. She licked her lips and spoke in a small voice. 'Yes, sir.'

The man's worn face gave a small smile. 'A young lady. What's your name?'

'Gerda, sir.'

'Gerda – a lovely name. Gerda, would you like to do something for the Fatherland? Something to help us win this war? Stop the bombs falling each night and set us free?'

Gerda stepped forward. 'Oh, yes, sir!'

'Are you a true German?'

'Yes, sir.'

'Then I can trust you with my secret,' the man said. 'I have a very secret message. It must be delivered now. But I am blind and weak. I need a nimble young person to run like the wind. Do you know Linden Street?'

'Yes, sir.'

'There is a shoe shop at number 27. Go in and tell the old cobbler that Hans sent you,' the soldier said. He reached into the pocket of the great grey overcoat and pulled out a crumpled envelope. 'And give him this. Whatever you do, you must not look in the envelope.'

'No, sir.'

'Good girl. Stop for no one, tell no one, trust no one. Now, run along before it gets dark!'

Gerda took the envelope, turned and ran through the empty streets past the shattered ruin of her old school and the splintered stumps of the trees in the park. The grass was mostly mud and her thin soles slipped as she sprinted across the park lawns. At the far side was the police station, an officer pulling the blackout curtains across watched her.

'Getting dark,' she panted. 'Must deliver the letter and get home before it gets dark.'

Then she stopped so suddenly her feet skidded on the cracked paving. She calmed herself, turned and walked into the police station. The weary old man behind the counter looked at her through red-rimmed eyes. 'Can I help?' he asked and though his thick grey moustache bristled fiercely his voice was kind.

Gerda told her story. The policeman nodded. 'I see,' he nodded. 'Suspicious.'

'That's what I thought!' she cried. 'I suddenly realized as I ran past here! How did he know it was getting dark if he was blind?'

The man picked up a cloak and threw it over his shoulders. 'I think I will take that note to number 27.'

It was later that night, as Gerda lay beneath a thin blanket and listened to the distant rumble of bombs that there was another rumble. Someone knocking at the door. Her mother showed the policeman into the house and Gerda sat up, wide-eyed, to listen. He told her what had happened.

'There is a cobbler shop at 27 Linden Street, run by an old man and his wife. When I went in the couple looked very nervous. Now all cobbler shops smell of sour old leather but the smell in that shop was worse. The man made an excuse and went through to the back shop. I heard the back door open then close and realized he'd escaped. So I looked around the shop and then I looked down in the cellar.'

244

'What was there?' Gerda asked and clutched at her mother's shawl.

'More horrors than I've seen in the whole of this terrible war,' the policeman groaned. 'There were bodies. Dead bodies. Most were cut up and wrapped like joints of meat to be sold to hungry customers.'

Gerda's mother gasped. 'I've heard of people eating human flesh.'

But Gerda had just one question. 'What was in the letter?'

The policeman passed it across to her. She unfolded the paper and read it…

Dear Jacob
This is the last one I shall be sending you today.
Your friend Hans

Gerda felt faint and giddy. 'I was…'

The policeman nodded. 'You were next.'

Well? A true story? Or just a wartime version of Red Riding Hood – the girl meeting the stranger who sends her off to be eaten?

Chilling for children

The Second World War was a young people's war. British and US soldiers could be as young as 18. Anyone in the British army aged 30 or over was called 'Dad'!

Teeny terrors

How do you make proper Nazis? Take children and train them. That was the aim of the Hitler Youth movement. But Adolf Hitler and the Nazis didn't invent the idea. At the end of the 1800s Herman Hoffman created the 'Wandervogel' – the German Youth Movement.

Wandervogel handbook

Rules:

Aims – German youths must discover nature.

Uniform – All members will wear dark shirts and shorts – even in the winter! It will do you good and it will help you discover nature.

Salute – when you meet another member of the movement you must raise your right arm in the air and cry 'Heil'.

In 1936 *all* German boys aged 15 to 18 had to join the Nazi Party Youth Organization – the Jugend (popularly known as the Hitler Youth). You would be called a 'Pimpf' and have to pass a test – sprint 50 metres in 12 seconds, take part in a two–day hike and recite their anthem, 'The Horst Wessel Song.' Wessel was a Nazi thug, killed in a street fight with Communists. The song cheered the Nazis by telling them the ghosts of dead Nazis were marching with them!

Once you'd passed the test you'd be given your Nazi knife with 'Blood and Honour' engraved on the blade. Boys aged 10 to 14 could practise being good Nazis by joining a junior Jugend – the Jungvolk – while ten-year-old girls joined the Jungmadel.

Gorgeous girls

The Nazis had a very clear idea of a perfect Nazi woman.

Attention Jungmadel!

Minister Joseph Goebbels has said: 'A woman has the task of being beautiful and bringing children into the world. The hen bird makes herself lovely for her mate and hatches her eggs for him.'

Will you grow to be a beautiful bird?

Remember! Good Nazi girls...

- wear their hair in a bun or plaits

- have blonde hair

- wear no make-up

- wear no lipstick

- do not smoke

- have broad hips

- and never wear trousers!

(You are also reminded that any girl under 18 caught smoking will be sentenced to two months in prison.)

Joseph Goebbels was keen on keeping girls in their place at the kitchen sink. He was Hitler's chief minister by the end of the war. He was weedy and had dark hair and skin so he was a long way from looking like the 'perfect' German he was trying to preserve.

When Hitler died he left the German state to Joseph Goebbels. Goebbels knew he was surrounded by advancing Soviet forces so he poisoned his six children – Helga, Heide, Hilde, Helmut, Holde and Hedda – poisoned his wife, and then himself. But for a few hours the man known as 'The Poisoned Dwarf'[1] was the Fuhrer of Germany – or at least of the few square yards that were all that was left of Nazi Germany.

Evacuees 1

German Children were evacuated from bombed cities and sent to camps run by loyal Nazi teachers or old soldiers. Military training was more important than studying. At one camp the children were encouraged to copy from each other rather than fail the exam. You may think that's a good idea and like to see it in your school! But before you suggest it to your head teacher you should be warned – there was a bad side to this camp's rules: if there was a speck of dust found in your room you'd be whipped.

1. He was also known as 'God's Mickey Mouse' – which is extremely cruel … to Mickey!

Evacuees 2

British children were evacuated to private houses in the countryside. But the city children were often very rough and their new country homes sometimes very posh.

One grand country lady complained to an evacuee's mother…

BUT HE DROPPED HIS TROUSERS AND HAD A POO IN THE MIDDLE OF THE CARPET

The mother grabbed the child, smacked him and reminded him…

BIFF

YOU DIRTY THING, MESSING UP THE LADY'S CARPET. WHY DIDN'T YOU DO IT IN THE CORNER LIKE I SHOWED YOU. EH?

Wee war workers

What *use* were the Hitler Youth? What did they actually *do*?

As the war went on, and older men and women died, the Hitler Youth replaced them. Roughly measured, in terms of coffin-power, the jobs became more dangerous and more disgusting.

TASK	DANGERS	RATING
1939 Deliver 'call-up' papers to soldiers, hand out ration cards, collect harvest, paint kerb-stones white to help with blackout (a popular job as it was paid!).	Being knocked over while painting curb or falling into a threshing machine while harvesting.	✝
1940 Door-to-door collection of materials such as paper, scrap metals, razor-blades, bottles, brass and copper.	Cutting yourself with a razor blade.	✝
1941 Girls sent to military hospitals to help nurses, to stations to serve food to soldiers and to nurseries to care for babies.	Catching some nasty infection from a wounded soldier or being bitten by a baby.	✝
1942 Joining anti-aircraft teams to shoot at enemy bombers and operate searchlights. These tasks were meant for boys over 15 but much younger boys and girls were used.	An all-girl unit shot down a US bomber over Vienna. The next bomber hit their position and killed three of them.	✝ ✝ BOOM

TASK	DANGERS	RATING
1943 The SS raise a fighting unit of 10,000 Hitler Youths over 16. Soldiers had a ration of cigarettes – Hitler Youth had a ration of sweets instead! (They hated that.)	Too young to smoke but old enough to die. When they went into action 6,000 were dead or wounded in the first month.	✝ ✝ ✝
1944 All boys over 16 forced to serve but many as young as 11 joined. An anti-tank gun could be handled easily by a boy.	A team of 12-year-olds who manned a large gun refused to surrender to the US army and were wiped out.	✝ ✝ ✝ ✝
1945 Hitler Youths called on to defend Germany as the Allies closed in. They dug trenches, fed refugees, nursed wounded, fought fires, rescued people from bomb-damaged buildings – and fought to the death.	At Oranienburg a Hitler Youth was put in charge of a group of soldiers even younger than himself. He decided to lead them home. The SS hanged him for deserting.	✝ ✝ ✝ ✝ ✝

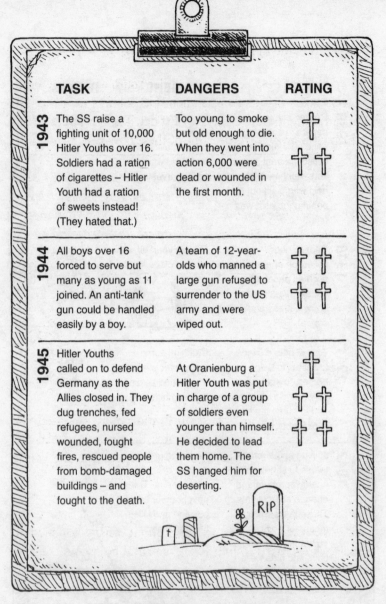

And when the war ended the horrors weren't over for the Hitler Youth members. They were treated by the Allies as

Nazis and made to help repair the damage of war.

On 30 April 1945, a group of Hitler Youth aged from ten to 14 were taken prisoner in Munich. US soldiers took them to Dachau concentration camp the next day. The boys were forced to help clear away the dead. One of these boys later wrote:

We were taken to a railway siding. We were ordered to open the freight cars... With metal bars we pushed back the doors. The skeleton of a woman fell out. After that nothing more, for the dead bodies were standing so close to one another, like sardines.

They were then taken to work in the crematorium!

Before the war the Hitler Youth movement sounded like bunches of boy scouts and gaggles of girl guides. Would you have wanted to join? And what happened to the young German people who *didn't* want to join?

Rotten for rebels

There's not a lot of information about what happened to rebels who refused to join Hitler's brutal boy scouts. There are some clues, though:

- It seemed that anyone caught enjoying themselves was guilty of wickedness. A shocked Hitler Youth report on a 'Swing Dance' (a bit like a disco today) revealed...

Date: February 1940

Report: Hamburg Swing Festival

The dance music was all English and American. The dancers made an appalling sight. Sometimes several couples formed a circle, linking arms and jumping, slapping hands, even rubbing the backs of their heads together. And then, bent double, with the top half of the body hanging loosely down, long hair flopping in the face, they dragged themselves round practically on their knees. Often boys could be seen dancing together, and each one had two cigarettes in the mouth, one in each corner...

- The German SS had a section to deal with 'youths' and a special 'youth concentration camp' was set up to deal with troublemakers. (You can be sure it would be worse than the worst detention your school could give you.)
- In 1942 Helmut Hulmut was arrested in Hamburg. What was Helmut Hulmut of Hamburg's crime? He was caught listening to BBC radio programmes! He also handed out anti-Nazi leaflets. His punishment? No, not tortured by being forced to listen to BBC Radio 2 for a week non-stop. But slightly worse. He was executed.
- Jonathan Stark was called to join the army in 1943. He refused to swear an oath to Hitler because Jonathan was a Jehovah's Witness. He was sent to Sachsenhausen camp and in 1944 the young Jon was hanged.

- There were groups of misfits who hung around coffee bars and dressed in clothes the Nazis did not approve of – checked shirts and battered hats – and even wore rings. These rebels called themselves daring names like 'The Black Gang' or 'The Edelweiss Pirates'. (Since 'Edelweiss' is a flower this must be a bit like calling your class football team 'The Poppy Pirates'. *That*'ll scare the opposition!) Groups like the Edelweiss Pirates sheltered German deserters and escaped prisoners of war, and even attacked the Gestapo. The Chief of the Cologne Gestapo was killed by the Pirates in autumn 1944.

The group members were arrested all over Germany. Lucky members were sent home with their heads shaved, unlucky ones were sent to the special youth concentration camps – and the leaders were hanged in public.

- In 1942 four teenagers put up anti-Nazi posters. You could be fined for this sort of thing today … so don't try this at home! But in 1942 Germany they were simply executed.

- Hans and Sophie Scholl founded the White Rose movement at Munich University to oppose the Nazis. Sophie discovered the ruthless way that Nazis exterminated disabled children while Hans saw brutal actions in the war against Russia. They met up in Munich in 1942 and painted 'Down with Hitler' on university walls. Then they gave out anti-Nazi leaflets – throwing dozens from university windows. They may as well have written, 'We want to be arrested by the SS' on the walls because they had no hope of getting away with it. Both were executed by guillotine.

Fighting small-fry

As the Germans became desperate for soldiers in 1944 there were 16-year-olds fighting on the front line. By the time the Soviets moved into Berlin in 1945 boys of 12 were defending the city.

A 12-year-old German boy found himself in a group of defenders...

I've no rifle. What should I do?

Cheer.

Blitzed Berlin

School rules can be boring. You want to chew gum in class? The school rules won't let you. You don't like rules. But when war comes rules can disappear. People make their own. Bullies take charge. That's when you'd be glad to see some rules!

A young German boy called Claus described what happened when war came close to Berlin in 1945. Some German soldiers fled, were captured by the German army and shot...

A few deserters, dressed only in underclothes, were dangling on a tree quite near our home. On their chests they had placards reading 'We betrayed the Fuhrer'.
The terror of our district was a small one-legged SS officer who stumped through the streets on crutches, a machine-pistol at the ready, followed by his men. Anyone he didn't like the look of he instantly shot.

The gang went down cellars and dragged all the men outside, giving them rifles and ordering them straight to the fighting. Anyone who hesitated was shot.

The front line was only a few streets away. Everything had run out. The only water was in the cellar of a house several streets away. To get bread one had to join a queue of hundreds, grotesquely adorned with steel helmets, outside the baker's shop at 3 a.m. At 5 a.m. the Soviet guns started. The crowded mass outside the shop pressed closely against the walls but no one moved from his place. Soviet low-flying planes machine-gunned people as they stood in their queues ... In every street dead bodies were left lying where they had fallen. Shopkeepers who had been jealously hoarding stocks not knowing how much longer they would be allowed to now began selling them. A burst of heavy shells tore to pieces hundreds of women who were waiting in the market hall.

Dead and wounded were flung on to wheelbarrows and carted away. The surviving women continued to wait. The Soviets drew nearer, they advanced with flame-throwers. Exhausted German soldiers would stumble in and beg for water. I remember one with a pale quivering face who said, 'We shall do it all right. We'll make our way to the north-west.' But his eyes belied his words. What he wanted to say was, 'Hide me. Give me shelter. I've had enough.' I should have liked to help him but neither of us dared speak. Each might have shot the other as a defeatist.

257

The Holocaust

The Nazis were a gang of bullies. And, like any gang of bullies, they needed victims. Adolf Hitler gave them people to hate. He told them to hate those he considered more animal than human. Who were these supposed sub-humans?

Soviets and Jews were top of the list.

The Nazis set about conquering the Soviets, taking control of their lands and using the survivors as slaves.

But the Nazis had a different plan for the Jews. Hitler's henchman, Heydrich, said:

We must exterminate the Jews wherever we find them.

This extermination became known as the 'Holocaust', which literally means wholly burnt.

'The Path to Heaven'

At first Jews were forced to dig pits, then they were shot and fell into the pits. But Hitler's head of extermination, Himmler, was worried…

We must have care and concern for our soldiers. Shooting Jews will upset them.

So the Nazis experimented with putting Jews into a sealed van and filling it with the exhaust gases from the van's engine. It took the victims eight minutes to die. Too slow.

At last they came up with the plan of using poisoned gas and they set up death camps to get rid of Jews at a much faster rate. One camp, Treblinka in the countryside of conquered Poland, saw the deaths of about one million people in 13 months. They were murdered by just 50 Germans with 150 Ukranian allies.

Of course the Nazis didn't tell the Jews, 'We're going to kill you.' If the Jews had known then they would have hidden or struggled or attacked the Nazis. Instead the Nazis told them lies from start to finish. They called the road to the gas chambers 'The Path to Heaven.' In fact it was the road to hell on earth.

Some Jews believed...   **The Nazis knew...**

① WE ARE BEING TAKEN FROM HOME TO TREBLINKA WORK CAMP

THEY ARE BEING TAKEN TO TREBLINKA DEATH CAMP

② AFTER THE WAR WE'LL GO TO A NEW HOMELAND FOR THE JEWS

THIS IS THE END OF THE WAR FOR THEM

③ THEY DON'T REALIZE THAT THE TRAIN IS SO CRAMPED AND AIRLESS THAT SOME PEOPLE DIE

IF THEY DIE ON THE TRAIN TO TREBLINKA THEN IT SAVES US THE TROUBLE OF KILLING THEM

From arriving at Treblinka station to being thrown into the burial pit would take about two hours – sometimes as little as an hour.

Escape from Hell

On 2 August 1943 the prisoners who were forced to help the exterminations in Treblinka carried out a plan to escape.

- A prisoner made a copy of the key to the gun store.
- The prisoners armed themselves.
- When they were sent to spray the wooden huts with disinfectant they put petrol in the sprayers.
- The huts were set alight.
- As the SS and the Ukranian guards fought the fire the prisoners fought their way out.
- 150 Jews escaped. Although about 100 Jews were recaptured, Treblinka was never rebuilt.

The Nazis tried to destroy the camps when they realized they were losing the war. But the site of Treblinka can still be seen to this day. The memorial stone on the spot says simply, 'Never again.'

Camp humour

One of the ways people survived the concentration camps was to turn the horror around them into humour. A popular Jewish joke in the camps went like this…

The Polish policeman's tale

War was an excuse for some people to act brutally. Today some football matches give hooligans a similar sort of excuse to break the rules, smash property and hurt people. But there are very few football hooligans in a crowd – and there are very few monsters even in a war.

There are more stories of individual courage than of cruelty. How would you have behaved in this situation?

1 The Germans conquered Poland in 1939, of course. But I was one who believed life was better under the Germans than the Soviets who were coming from the west. I had served in Warsaw as a policeman before the war. When the Germans arrived I kept my job and simply said:

2 The Germans gathered the Jews into one area of the city where they could keep their eye on them – the ghetto. My job was to make sure they stayed there. I never liked the Jews myself and they never liked me. From time to time we would go into the ghetto, take out the strongest and send them to the labour camps.

YOU WILL BE WORKING FOR THE GOOD OF POLAND

3 Even when I heard the stories of Jews being gassed I tried to ignore them. But we all knew that when someone went off to the camps they were never seen again. Soon there were only women and children left in the ghetto. Then one day the German military commander gave us an order.

MY MEN ARE GOING TO ROUND UP THE WOMEN AND CHILDREN. YOU LOYAL POLISH POLICE ARE GOING TO ASSIST. YOU KNOW THE AREA

4 It was true. The houses were like a rats' nest – corridors and stairways and cellars and tunnels where they hid when they knew we were coming. We Polish police knew them best. This raid was to be planned in secrecy. The Jews would have no time to escape. We would seal their secret routes and

263

then drag them out. In the early hours, when they would all be sleeping, we went into the ghetto.

5 But someone had warned them. When we broke down the flimsy doors to their rooms the same sight greeted us.

6 The German Commandant ordered us to search the buildings from cellar to attic. The Commandant himself came along with me. He knew that if anyone could find the Jews it was me. We climbed through the house and I opened every secret panel and trapdoor that I knew about. Every one was empty. At last we reached the top of the house. A ladder led down from a gap in the ceiling.

7 So I took a lantern and began climbing the long ladder. The silence was so great I couldn't believe anyone could be up there in the space below the rafters. But I climbed on. At last I reached the entrance to the loft. If anyone was waiting they could have smashed my head in there and then. I looked over the lip of the hole and shone the lantern in. The light picked out the white faces and wide, dark eyes of 20 women and terrified children. The Commander called up to me.

8 The reward for taking so many Jews would be great, I knew. I'd be promoted. I'd be a loyal and trusted servant of our conquerors and I would share in their power and wealth. I turned to the Commander and called back down.

Well? What would you have done? You know you'll be sending those women and children to their deaths, but this is war. Thousands are dying every day. What's another 20? And your own wife and family must come first.

What did that Polish policeman do?

The gentle German

The war wasn't a simple matter of 'good' Allies against 'evil' Nazis. Sometimes the British were known to execute children and many Nazis were known to spare them.

A Jewish mother faced a Lithuanian soldier, working for the Nazis. The Lithuanian raised his gun and pointed it at her head. His finger tightened on the trigger. He was about to kill her for the 'crime' of being Jewish.

Suddenly a German Army officer stepped forward and rescued her. He turned to the soldier and explained:

One day history will judge us.

History *has* judged the Nazis and generally they have been found 'guilty' – but not all of them.

The woman and her three children survived the war. They lived in a hole under the floor of a barn for almost a year. The hole was about the size of a table. They were four of the 30 survivors in their town. Before the war there had been 25,000.

Epilogue

On 3 September 1939 the *Washington Post* newspaper had a headline that read:

BOTH SIDES AGREE NOT TO BOMB CIVILIANS

Six years later the United States dropped the most horrifying bombs yet invented on the towns of Hiroshima and Nagasaki in Japan.

What changed in those six years? People changed. The world had seen so many horrors that thousands of innocent civilian deaths seemed worthwhile if it meant a quick end to the war.

In 1939 most people really believed that wars were fought only by soldiers. The Second World War changed that for ever. Wars were being fought by everyone; people in the cities as well as men on the battlefields.

An American said, 'Total wars are won by the side with the biggest factories.'

MY FACTORY IS BIGGER THAN YOUR FACTORY!

In the Second World War it had become easier to kill someone when all you had to do was push a button and drop a bomb. You'd never see the suffering you caused. But the real horror of the war was that so many people were prepared to kill so many others in cold blood. A screaming child, a weeping woman or a feeble old man – the killers often showed not one drop of pity. That's what war can do to ordinary people.

They are the things that make the Second World War the most horrible history of all: the innocence of the victims, the vast numbers of them and the unbelievable cruelty of some of the fighters.

That's why truly horrible history can be so important. It helps us to look back at the horror and say the single word from the memorial at the destroyed village of Oradour-sur-Glane:

REMEMBER

WHY IS IT THAT THE ONES WHO MOST NEED TO REMEMBER ARE THE ONES MOST LIKELY TO FORGET?

WOEFUL
SECOND WORLD
WAR

GRISLY QUIZ

**Now find out if you're a Woeful
Second World War expert!**

SECOND WORLD WAR WONDERS

Try this quick quiz on the Second World War. Replace the words 'Laurel and Hardy'* with one of the answers below. One of those answers is 'Laurel and Hardy'!

The missing words in the wrong order are: uniforms, 16-year-old boys, Laurel and Hardy, bonfires, nuns, toilet rolls, women, prison, parachutes, guillotines.

1. British and Allied troops coloured everything khaki brown as camouflage. They even had khaki *Laurel and Hardy*.

2. The British Home Guard were warned that an enemy paratrooper might be disguised as *Laurel and Hardy*.

3. Some spies in Germany were executed by *Laurel and Hardy*.

4. British soldiers in Italy were given summer *Laurel and Hardy* and some died of the cold.

5. In November 1940 a man called Lloyd was arrested in Britain for having *Laurel and Hardy* in his back garden.

6. US paratroopers were safer than British ones because they had two *Laurel and Hardy*.

7. The Germans sent *Laurel and Hardy* into battle when they became short of soldiers.

8. The Nazis thought ideal *Laurel and Hardy* should have broad hips.

* If you're not old enough to know who Laurel and Hardy are, then ask your teacher or a parent.

9. Workers who were late for work in a German factory ended up in *Laurel and Hardy*.

10. Italian leader Mussolini was said to look like one half of *Laurel and Hardy*.

WELL THIS WAR IS CERTAINLY KEEPING US BUSY OLLIE!

QUICK QUESTIONS

1. When the Second World War started in 1939 civilians were urged to join the Local Defence Volunteers. Comedians said LDV stood for Look, Duck and … what? (Clue: Vanquish? Not quite.)

2. In May 1940 Mr Hitler did something a certain Mr Fawkes failed to do. What? (Clue: remember?)

3. In 1940 a man was arrested for lighting a cigarette. Why? (Clue: night-light)

4. The British government tried to ban Londoners sheltering in the Underground stations during bombing raids. What did the crafty Cockneys do? (Clue: train for it)

5. Car headlights were masked because of the blackout. How did farmers protect their black cattle that may have strayed on to the road? (Clue: zebra crossing?)

6. Why did parents have to label every piece of their children's clothing during the war? (Clue: bits and pieces)

7. During the war, the tops of pillar-boxes were painted green or yellow. Why? (Clue: it's a gas)

8. When the war ended in 1945 some children tried to eat bananas without peeling them. Why? (Clue: Yes! We have no bananas!)

9. In the 1940s you could eat 'chicken fruit on bacon ducks'. What was it?
a) boiled beef and carrots
b) omelette with sun dried tomatoes
c) eggs on fried bread

10. During the Second World War, US soldiers were advised to eat…
a) caterpillars
b) maggots
c) absolutely anything

MORE CATERPILLAR CASSEROLE PLEASE

WAR-LIKE WORDS?

At the end of the millennium, people were still bombing and killing but they'd found some new words to describe it so that it sounded less horrible. See if you can work out what these military phrases mean.

Words	Meaning
1. air support	a) human beings
2. friendly fire	b) destroy
3. neutralizing	c) planes dropping bombs
4. soft targets	d) blowing people to pieces by mistake
5. collateral damage	e) assassinating a human nuisance
6. immobilize	f) shooting soldiers on your own side

THESE DAYS YOU NEED GUNS, TANKS, SMART BOMBS AND A DICTIONARY

Answers

Second World War Wonders

1. Toilet rolls. A quick flash of white could give them away to the enemy!

2. Nuns. Or vicars or a woman carrying a baby.

3. Guillotines. In August 1942 German spy-catchers uncovered a team of 46 spies. The male spies were hanged, but for some reason the female spies were guillotined.

4. Uniforms. The army planners believed it would be very hot in Italy, but it was wet and cold and in the mountains it was freezing.

5. Bonfires. Mr Lloyd supported the Nazi party. The magistrate gave Lloyd a prison sentence – Lloyd gave the magistrate a Nazi salute.

6. Parachutes. The British Army said two parachutes took up too much room. The truth was probably that it would have been too expensive.

7. 16-year-old boys. As the war went on and the fit men were killed or captured the German Army called for older men and younger boys to join.

8. Women. The ideal Nazi woman should also have blonde hair, never wear make-up or trousers, and wear her hair in a bun or plaits.

9. Prison. You could be sentenced to three months in prison. (And you thought an hour's detention for being late to school was cruel!)

10. Laurel and Hardy. Mussolini was short and fat. When he became ruler of Italy he wore a dark suit and a bowler hat. Somebody told him he looked just like Oliver Hardy – a comic idiot – so he began dressing in military uniforms instead.

Quick Questions

1. Vanish. The LDV went on to become the Home Guard, popularly known as 'Dad's Army'.

2. His bombs flattened the Houses of Parliament.

3. He was breaking the blackout laws in force during the war.

4. They bought platform tickets so no one could stop them going down to safety.

5. They painted white stripes down their sides.

6. If the child was blown to pieces then the bits could be identified. Gruesome but true-some.

7. So that droplets of deadly mustard gas would stain the paint and show if there was a gas attack.

8. Many children had never seen a banana and didn't know what to do with it.

9.c)

10.b) A US Army handbook advised them to eat maggots and grasshoppers (with the wings and legs removed!), but advised against eating caterpillars.

War-like words
1.c) 2.f) 3.e) 4.a) 5.d) 6.b)

INTERESTING INDEX

Where will you find 'exploding dogs', 'knickers' and
'torn-out toe nails' in an index? In a Horrible Histories
book, of course!

Terry **Deary** was born at a very early age, so long ago he can't remember. But his mother, who was there at the time, says he was born in Sunderland, north-east England, in 1946 – so it's not true that he writes all *Horrible Histories* from memory. At school he was a horrible child only interested in playing football and giving teachers a hard time. His history lessons were so boring and so badly taught, that he learned to loathe the subject. *Horrible Histories* is his revenge.

Martin **Brown** was born in Melbourne, on the proper side of the world. Ever since he can remember he's been drawing. His dad used to bring back huge sheets of paper from work and Martin would fill them with doodles and little figures. Then, quite suddenly, with food and water, he grew up, moved to the UK and found work doing what he's always wanted to do: drawing doodles and little figures.

HORRIBLE HISTORIES

HAVE YOU
GOT THE WHOLE
HORRIBLE LOT?

ISBN 978 1407 10428 7

ISBN 978 0439 94403 8

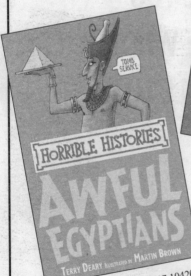

ISBN 978 1407 10420 1

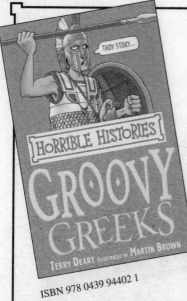

ISBN 978 0439 94402 1

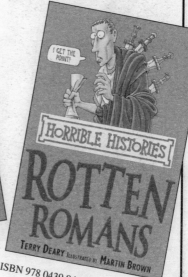

ISBN 978 0439 94400 7

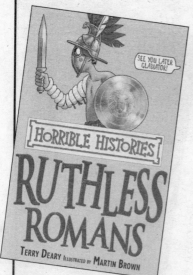

ISBN 978 1407 10424 9

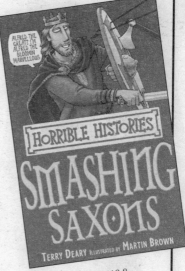

ISBN 978 1407 10418 8

ISBN 978 1407 10430 0

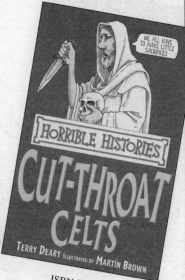

ISBN 978 1407 10426 3

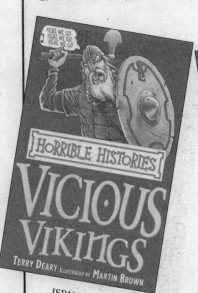

ISBN 978 0439 94406 9

ISBN 978 0439 94401 4

ISBN 978 1407 10425 6

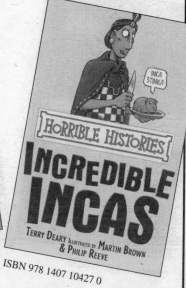

ISBN 978 1407 10427 0

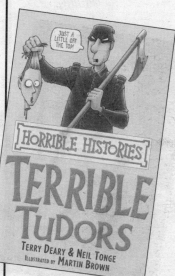

ISBN 978 0439 94405 2

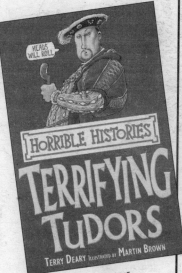

ISBN 978 1407 10422 5

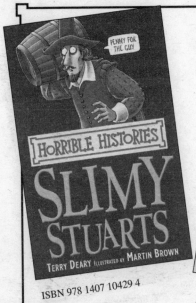

ISBN 978 1407 10429 4

ISBN 978 1407 10419 5

ISBN 978 0439 94404 5

ISBN 978 1407 10431 7